PARTICIPANT BOOK

DAVID

God's Shepherd, Warrior, and King

FREDERICK J. GAISER

Augsburg Fortress
Minneapolis

Contents

TABLE OF CONTENTS

DAVID
God's Shepherd, Warrior, and King

This Participant Book has a corresponding Leader Guide.

Editors: Katherine A. Evensen and Carolyn F. Lystig

Designer: Koechel Peterson & Associates Inc.

Photo credits: cover—photo compositions, Koechel Peterson & Associates: statue of David © Image Club Graphics, shepherd, Koechel Peterson & Associates; p. 5, 59—Foto Marburg / Art Resource; p. 8—Image Club Graphics; pp. 11, 55—Alinari / Art Resource; p. 16—Mimi Forsyth; p. 25—Jewish Museum / Art Resource; pp. 35, 41—The Pierpont Morgan Library / Art Resource; p. 49—Unicorn Stock Photos/Wayne Floyd.

Illustration credits: p. 15—Leonard Baskin; p. 17—*The New Oxford Annotated Bible;* p. 22—Dana Fradon; p. 28—Gahan Wilson; pp. 45, 60—Tanja Butler.

ISBN 0-8066-3364-6

Manufactured in U.S.A.

1 2 3 4 5 6 7 8 9 0 1 2 3 4 5 6 7 8 9

PB = Participant Book
LG = Leader Guide

Introduction 3
Series Overview 3
Course Overview 4

1 The Promise of Youth 5
1 Samuel 16:1-23; Psalm 8:1-9

2 The Promise of Success 15
2 Samuel 5:1-25; Psalm 18:1-50

3 The Promise of a House 25
2 Samuel 7:1-29; Psalm 132:1-18

4 A Breach of Promise 35
2 Samuel 11:1-27; Psalm 51:1-19

5 The Promised Shepherd 45
1 Samuel 17:1-58; Psalm 23:1-6

6 The Hope of Promise 55
1 Kings 1:1-53; Psalm 144:1-15

Acknowledgments—SESSION 1: *Samuel Anointing David* engraving from Foto Marburg/Art Resource, NY. Used by permission of Art Resource; *Statue of King David* from Alinari/Art Resource, NY. Used by permission of Art Resource; "God Who Stretched the Spangled Heavens" by Catherine Cameron, copyright © 1967 Hope Publishing Co., Carol Stream IL 60188. All rights reserved. Used by permission. SESSION 2: *A Passover Haggadah* © 1982, reprinted by permission of Central Conference of American Rabbis; Map 9 "Jerusalem in Old Testament" from *The New Oxford Annotated Bible* edited by Bruce Metzger and Herbert May, copyright © 1973, 1977, 1991 Oxford University Press, Inc. Used by permission; Cartoon by Dana Fradon © 1994 The New Yorker Collection. All rights reserved. Used by permission. SESSION 3: *Prayer at the Temple of Jerusalem* from Jewish Museum/Art Resource, NY. Used by permission of Art Resource; Cartoon by Gahan Wilson © 1986 The New Yorker Collection. All rights reserved. Used by permission. SESSION 4: *David and Bathsheba* and *David and Jonathan Meet* from The Pierpont Morgan Library/Art Resource, NY. Used by permission of Art Resource. SESSION 5: Linocut by Tanja Butler from *Graphics for Worship* © 1996 Augsburg Fortress; *Jesus the Good Shepherd* photo credit: Unicorn Stock Photos/Wayne Floyd. SESSION 6: Prayer of the Day for Christ the King, © 1978 *Lutheran Book of Worship*; *The Temple of Solomon,* Reconstruction Drawing, from Foto Marburg/Art Resource, NY. Used by permission of Art Resource; Linocut by Tanja Butler from *Graphics for Worship* © 1996 Augsburg Fortress; Prayer from *Rite of Christian Initiation of Adults,* © 1985 International Committee on English in the Liturgy, Inc. (ICEL); "Bright and Glorious is the Sky" stanza 6, © 1958 *Service Book and Hymnal.*

Introduction

SERIES OVERVIEW

WELCOME

Welcome to the Inspire Bible Study Series. The courses in this series invite you to be inspired through study of the Word. Conversations with other participants, and with those who have considered these texts through the centuries, will open your heart and mind to the Spirit. Expect to be motivated and strengthened by the Spirit to grow in faith and to put your faith into action—to serve and inspire others.

SERIES OBJECTIVES

The Inspire courses will help participants and leaders:

- deepen their knowledge and understanding of the Bible;
- explore biblical and theological scholarship;
- study and discuss biblical, historical, and contemporary forms of the salvation story;
- witness to the gospel;
- continue to seek ways to nurture their faith.

INSPIRE COURSES

Genesis: *Creation, Choices, and Consequences*

Exodus: *God's Exodus People*

Life in the Promised Land: *God's People from Generation to Generation*

David: *God's Shepherd, Warrior, and King*

Psalms: *Find Yourself in the Psalms*

Jeremiah: *God Calls a Servant*

The Gospel of Mark: *God's Grace in Action*

The Gospel of John: *Conversations with Jesus*

Acts: *See God's Amazing Grace*

Romans: *New Life in Christ Jesus*

The Pastoral Epistles: *Keeping Faith Alive in a Changing World*

Revelation: *Images of Hope*

INSPIRE PARTICIPANTS

Inspire Bible Study Series is designed for adults like you who are interested in an in-depth study of the Bible. The approach and material in this study is designed for those who:

- will read the material in the participant book before each session;
- bring a variety of learning styles, experiences, gifts, and questions to the class;
- expect to participate actively in their learning;
- are familiar with the Bible;
- have had experience in Christian education groups for adults;
- study the Bible as a resource for making decisions in daily life based on their own understanding and practice of their relationship with God;
- are looking for ways to share the gospel with others;
- expect that, as a result of their commitment and effort, they will be changed and will make a difference in the lives of others.

The leader is both teacher and participant. In the role of teacher, the leader will plan the session, guide the process, and facilitate discussion. As a participant, the leader will explore with you ways the living Word of God addresses our lives today.

BIBLE TRANSLATIONS

Inspire Bible Study Series uses the New Revised Standard Version Bible (NRSV) as the primary text. When the writer has used another translation, that translation is identified. You are encouraged to use a translation of the Bible (as opposed to a paraphrase). Having available more than one translation of the Bible can enhance the discussion of a particular text.

> *Inspire* means "to breathe life into" or "to move or guide by divine influence."

REFERENCE TOOLS

As you read the Bible, you will have questions about the text. A library of available reference material will enhance your study. Here are the most common types of helps:

- **Annotated** or study Bible (*The New Oxford Annotated Bible: New Revised Standard Version; NRSV Harper Study Bible; HarperCollins Study Bible,* 15 vols.);
- Bible **commentary** (*Augsburg Commentary on the New Testament, 15 vols.; Harper's Bible Commentary; The Women's Bible Commentary; The New Jerome Biblical Commentary*);
- Bible **concordance** (*The Concise Concordance to the New Revised Standard Version; The NRSV Concordance Unabridged*);
- Bible **handbook** (*The Oxford Companion to the Bible*);
- Bible **dictionary** (*Theological Dictionary of the New Testament; Anchor Bible Dictionary, 6 vols.; The Interpreter's Dictionary of the Bible,* 5 vols.);
- Bible **atlas** (*Oxford Bible Atlas,* Third Edition).

GETTING READY

This book is for you. As you prepare for each session, read all the materials that are provided. Your Bible study group might only have time to reference some of this information. However, your Bible study journey will be enhanced by everything you find here.

COURSE OVERVIEW

COURSE OBJECTIVES

This course will help the participants and leader:

- explore God's saving grace within the context of the joys and frailty of human existence;
- connect David's story with their own journey of faith;
- celebrate and give witness to God's enduring love and faithfulness.

NOTE: As you read literature that dates ancient times, you may note that often "B.C.E." or "C.E." appear where you would expect to see "B.C." or "A.D." "B.C." means "before Christ"; and "A.D." is the abbreviation for the Latin phrase "anno Domini" meaning "year of the Lord." Christians have used these abbreviations to date world history in reference to Christ's presence on earth. Many Jews and other non-Christians quite appropriately have raised concerns about this practice. As a sign of respect for the common root yet separate branches of Judaism and Christianity, many scholars have switched to the abbreviations "B.C.E." (before the Common Era) and "C.E." (Common Era). The "Common Era" refers to time shared by Jews and Christians—exactly the same time previously indicated by "A.D." Correspondingly, "B.C.E." refers to the time previously indicated "B.C."

COURSE FOCUS

The biblical books of history tell us much of David's story. The psalms recount his faith and his moods. Together they provide us a full and vibrant, sometimes stirring, sometimes troubling, picture of this shepherd, warrior, and king.

Session 1—David enters the stage of Israel's history as the ideal young man, the ruler of promise, anointed with God's spirit.

Session 2—David is made king of all Israel and experiences military and political success. In this chapter of David's life, there is a purity that ascribes victory to God with a confident and thankful heart.

Session 3—David seeks to honor God by building him a "house"—a temple in Jerusalem. However, we are reminded that the future lies in God's hands, not ours.

Session 4—David's personal life reveals his—and our—human frailty and need for divine guidance and forgiveness.

Session 5—The dangers David meets as a shepherd prepare him for combat with Goliath, the "giant" of the Philistines. Shepherd images play an important role in the life of David. They set the stage for the New Testament's introduction of Jesus as the Good Shepherd.

Session 6—David's last days as a weak old man lead us to wonder where hope finally lies in our long story. Hope emerges, however, in the God who keeps his promises, who works in every generation to establish his messianic rule. That promise comes down even to us through Jesus, the Lord's Messiah.

BACKGROUND

The story of David stretches through the books of 1 and 2 Samuel and culminates in the first two chapters of 1 Kings. Although most Christians know something about David, many have not worked through the biblical details of his life. It is a rich and troublesome journey.

David is an exciting and charismatic figure, attracting attention immediately as he comes on the scene of Old Testament history. He is a genuine hero, and the early stories have a heroic, almost legendary, character. This hero quickly becomes enmeshed in the political struggles and wars that marked early Israelite history. Usually successful, he grew in power and influence, ascribing his victories to God and singing God's praises.

Trouble looms on David's horizon, however, especially in his familial and personal relationships. He breaks his trust with other people and with God. Were it not for God's ongoing commitment to David, his promise to maintain David's "house" or royal line, David would certainly not enjoy the favor with which he is remembered by later biblical tradition. God, it seems, must hold on to David in spite of David. But God does hold on, and David's house becomes the model and source of the biblical idea of a messianic ruler. New Testament believers will eventually welcome Jesus as the son of David.

We cannot understand David without hearing his songs alongside his story. These are recorded for us in the book of Psalms. They include his great hymns of victory, his cries of distress in times of trouble, his humiliation as a repentant sinner, his royal hopes, his trust in God, and his concern for God's people.

Make the Most of this Study

- Take time before each session to read the session's core Bible text(s) and participant material.
- Participate actively in each session by sharing your thoughts, convictions and experiences. Listen carefully to others.
- Look at the "Session Bridge" section of each session for at-home activities that help you review the work you have done and prepare for the next session.
- Keep a personal journal of your thoughts, questions, and insights while you immerse yourself for six weeks in this study. An Inspire Journal is available for this purpose.

Session ONE

the promise of YOUTH

EXPERIENCES & REFLECTIONS

FOCUS David enters the stage of Israel's history as the ideal young man, the ruler of promise, anointed with God's spirit.

Samuel Anointing David Julius Schnorr von Carolsfeld

Prayer

Creator God, you made all people a little lower than the angels—not only David, but us as well. As you once sent your spirit upon David, send it now upon us and upon all who seek to govern your world that we and they might work with you to bring peace and harmony on earth. Give us hope, Lord God, in Jesus' name. Amen.

NAME AND REFLECT

A time to hope! A moment of promise! The inauguration of a popular new president can be such a moment. Parades and speeches, honor guards and VIPs, inaugural balls and fireworks—everything announces that something important is happening, something new. Perhaps it can all work this time!

Another moment of promise is the installation of a new pastor. Hymns and readings, choirs and handbells, sermons and ceremony—everything suggests that both congregation and God have a big investment here. New ministry promises new life for the congregation and its community.

SESSION 1

1 Samuel 16:1-23; Psalm 8:1-9

Allow yourself to daydream for a minute. Where would you like an "ideal" leader to take your county or your congregation? What characteristics would your "ideal" leader have?

BRING IT *together*

In biblical Israel, "church" and "state" were essentially one. Do you think this means that God was more active in the life of the state in those days than in the present? Was there more or less reason for Israel in the time of David to be optimistic about its future than we are? Why or why not?

THE TEXT SPEAKS

START WITH THE BIBLE

"Skillful in playing, a man of valor, a warrior, prudent in speech, and a man of good presence; and the LORD is with him" (1 Samuel 16:18).

This is the Bible's introduction to David. If these words were written by a candidacy committee to introduce a potential pastor or associate in ministry, they would gain the attention of any congregation. Translated into present language, the description might read: "The candidate is artistic and creative, a person of courage and integrity; she is articulate and gives good account of herself; most important, she is a faithful believer in whom we discern God's own call to ministry."

The candidate is artistic and creative, a person of courage and integrity; she is articulate and gives good account of herself; most important, she is a faithful believer in whom we discern God's own call to ministry.

Reading the Bible, we become as intrigued with David as a congregation might become with the ideal contemporary candidate: "This guy looks promising!" Our study will pursue more deeply the nature of David's promise. According to Scripture, what will an ideal leader look like?

EXPLORE THE TEXT

The Bible introduces us to David in two bodies of material: the stories of Samuel, Kings, and Chronicles and the songs of the book of Psalms. This double insight into a biblical character is rare, and we want to make use of it. Our study, therefore, will look at David in both song and story. Each David story will be linked with a psalm—one associated in the Psalter with David—that amplifies the message of the session. In this session, both 1 Samuel 16 and Psalm 8 celebrate aspects of an ideal humanity under God.

What Kind of Story?

How would you introduce a great leader? Would we hire Abraham Lincoln as our lawyer more quickly if we read a formal résumé listing important dates, educational background, and professional assessments or if we heard stories about his log-cabin origins and legendary honesty?

Scripture chooses stories rather than data to introduce David. That doesn't mean biographical and historical data are not important. In fact, demonstrating clearly that Jesus derives from the "house and family of David" will be exceedingly important to the New Testament (Matthew 1:1-17; Luke 2:4). But for now, to draw us into David's life, the author of 1 Samuel uses personal, even playful, stories rather than objective history. Biblical truth, like modern truth, comes in a variety of forms. Stories can be at least as true as histories, sometimes more true. In the beginning, with David, we get stories.

We could, in fact, compare this biblical introduction to David to fairy tales or heroic legends. We know the type—children's literature is full of them—where the hero turns out to be the completely unexpected one: the ugly duckling or the unlikely lad who pulls a sword out of a stone and is pronounced king. David was something like that, says our text, at first unworthy of consideration by human standards, but marked by a much more important feature: the Lord was with him.

The Lord Was with Him

Whatever else is true about David, he is God's choice. Both form and content of the text leave no doubt. The first story in 1 Samuel 16, the selection of David from the sons of Jesse, is surrounded by references to the "horn of oil" (verses 1 and 13). The oil will be used for the anointing, to mark David as God's own king. Anointing someone to power was the Old Testament equivalent of administering our oath of office. It was formal, it was visible, it was irretractable. In Tom Clancy's novel *Executive Orders,* a pretender to the presidency will turn up and cause trouble, but Jack Ryan has taken the oath. He is and remains POTUS (President of the United States). In 1 Samuel, it is not yet clear *how* David will assume the throne, but there is no doubt *that* he will be king. He has been anointed. Like Arthur, he has "pulled the sword from the stone."

The second story in the chapter, David's arrival at the court of Saul, is surrounded by references to an "evil spirit" tormenting Saul (verses 14 and 23). Choosing David necessarily means rejecting Saul. The transition from the first to the second story is as clear as it is disturbing: at the close of part one, "the spirit of the LORD came mightily upon David" (verse 13); at the beginning of part two, "the spirit of the LORD departed from Saul" (verse 14). Worse, the "evil spirit" itself was "from the LORD." Without apology, the author claims that this shift in power is God's doing. It is not merely an accident of politics and history.

This claim of divine participation does not mean that "secular" historians could make no sense of this period. They can and do, giving a variety of reasons for the rise of David and the decline of Saul. The biblical view does not require a choice between divine involvement and human effort. God truly works in the world; but God works in and through real human history. Still, the biblical writers are usually more direct than we would be in describing what God is up to.

Even in the surprising rejection of Saul, God does not, however, act capriciously in these stories. God does not act without cause or without reference to a broader goal or sense of purpose. As the ongoing study will clarify, God chooses David not for David's sake, but for Israel's (and ours). Under Saul, things were going wrong. History needed a new start; God made a new start. Yet, even God's rejection of Saul as king does not imply God's disinterest in Saul as human. In one of the chapter's most poignant features, the same David who will supplant a disobedient Saul on the throne is the one who, sent by God, is able to provide a tormented Saul with human love (verse 21) and release from anxiety (verse 23).

> [David's] popular following, his victories over the Philistines and others, and his establishment of a powerful kingdom show him to have been a shrewd military strategist and motivator.... Administratively, his establishment of the military, civil, and religious bureaucracies displayed yet another dimension of his talents. David's skills as a poet, musician, and sponsor of music were renowned as well.... Ultimately, however, David's lasting significance lay in his position as YHWH's chosen king for Israel and as the father of the dynasty that YHWH chose to bless.[1]
>
> —David M. Howard, Jr.
>
> *Note:* YHWH are the four consonants representing the ancient Hebrew name for God, commonly referred to today as Yahweh or Jehovah.

Do Appearances Matter?

Whether or not appearances matter depends upon whether you listen to your therapist (Not primarily!) or to a TV commercial for jeans or hair dye (Absolutely!). Intriguingly, our text seems to say both things. Human beings, we learn, "look on the outward appearance, but the LORD looks on the heart" (verse 7). The oldest son might have the height and the looks—and certainly, in that culture, the first right to leadership and power—but these are not the primary criteria. God's choice will be based not on cultural norms that favor external appearance and the prevailing social order; God's choice will look on the heart. In some ways, Paul's much later observation applies already here: God will choose "what is weak in the world to shame the strong" (1 Corinthians 1:27).

David Michalengelo (1475–1564)

Still, when we meet David we learn that he is "ruddy," has "beautiful eyes," and is "handsome" (1 Samuel 16:12). More, he is "skillful in playing, a man of valor, a warrior, prudent in speech, and a man of good presence" (verse 18). Today we might say that David is "lookin' good." Are these not matters of appearance?

In the biblical world, as in ours, it will apparently be useful for a leader to have qualities associated with leadership: courage, creativity, social and natural graces, intelligence, even a little pizazz. Whether serving on a call committee or voting for a president, we would not regard such things as irrelevant. Nevertheless, the text reminds us that there are things of greater importance—things of the heart. No pastor, no president can rest on appearances alone. Some try (so will David!), but the results are disastrous.

Once again, our text is rich and nuanced and true. To say that external things don't matter, but internal things do, would be too simplistic for our text. The world is real. God gives people different talents. Certain gifts enhance leadership. Nevertheless, without God at the center, people and leaders and history itself will fail. Not only that, but the God whom we find in the center of things in the Bible is one who surprises. True, David has real gifts of leadership, but we are surprised to find them there. He is after all, the little kid, the one left out to take care of the sheep because somebody has to do the chores while the grown-ups concern themselves with things that matter. He is the social underling who ought not be heard from until power has trickled down through the ranks. But God can change the ranks or disregard them. God has a way of surprising us with leaders we did not expect, leaders graced with real authority and talent but unexpected all the same. God begins a new period in Israel's history with a new, young, ideal, but unexpected, David.

Diagnosing Saul

Saul's illness and decline are not our primary interest in this session. However, the "evil spirit from the LORD" (verse 14) probably torments many of us almost as much as it did Saul. It torments us because most of us have been taught to interpret "spells" that cause a person to be depressed (verse 23) or to rave and strike out (1 Samuel 18:10-11) as illness rather than as possession or evil—and certainly not as an "evil" sent by God. What does this mean?

Again, the Bible is blunt in its attribution of events to God. The world of the Bible was, no doubt, much more directly theistic than the modern western world. God was involved in what happened. The Bible never claims that everything that happens is the will of God; nor does it imply that God's work permits no human responsibility or rational explanation. But it does insist that God is at work.

A western diagnosis of mental illness for Saul need not exclude a theological interpretation of these events. Even if, from our perspective, Saul's problem can be called illness, what is God doing in this illness? People of God will rightly ask such questions, just as they did in the Bible. Different people and different times will explain events differently; but their explanations, no matter how detailed or how valid, cannot and need not exclude God from the picture.

Even now, non-Western cultures will have much less trouble with this text. Of course spirits are at work in the world, many of them will say. Of course illness and health are related to a person's relation to God. Questions of worldview—modern or ancient, Western or non-Western—are not irrelevant. Respectfully investigated, they can provide meat for rich human conversation. Disagreements will be inevitable. However, no human worldview can either explain God out of history or prove God into history. Seeing God at work is a matter of faith, for people in any place or in any age and regardless of how they explain events in the world. Our text sees God at work in the lives of Saul and David. As people of God, we listen and are prepared to learn and to talk of God's work in our world in the language of our century.

What Are Human Beings?

Psalm 8 is one of the many biblical psalms associated with David. The king in the psalm—the ruler or sovereign—is God. Thinking about God and God's incredible creation produces wonder and awe among humans, even a sense of overwhelming insignificance: "What are human beings that you are mindful of them?" (verse 4).

Most often in the Bible such a question triggers a negative answer. Humans "are like a breath; their days are like a passing shadow" (Psalm 144:4). In Job, things are worse. Bildad, too, ponders creation and declares humans to be "maggots" and "worms" (Job 25:6). There may be such moments for Job, for Shakespeare, and for us, but not for David, at least not in Psalm 8. Humans are nothing less than God's coworkers in the world, "crowned … with glory and honor" (Psalm 8:5). The psalm shares the optimism of 1 Samuel 16. God is making a new beginning. David is the ideal ruler; humans are the crown of creation. All things are possible!

Little Less than *What*?

Translations vary in Psalm 8:5. Are humans made "a little lower than God" (NRSV) or "little lower than the angels" (KJV)? Perhaps the distinction is not so important. The Hebrew term *ELOHIM* can refer to God or to the "heavenly beings." However the verse is translated, the reference is clear: the text remembers with Genesis 1 that humans are created in the image of God. The move in the psalm from the heavens to humans to dominion over the earth follows exactly the line of direction of Genesis 1. The basis for the psalm's optimistic view of human beings and human possibility is the fact of our creation in the image of God. God began a new thing in Genesis 1; God begins a new thing with David; God can begin new things with us. We are little lower than the angels.

Thinking about God and God's incredible creation produces wonder and awe among humans, even a sense of overwhelming insignificance: "What are human beings that you are mindful of them?" (Psalm 8:4).

A Song for Our Time?

Are human beings really "a little lower than God"? Or, if we were once, are we still? The trouble with reading the David story as the beginning of a new ideal government, a Camelot where all things are possible, is that most of us have read it before. We know that David, like King Arthur in Camelot, will soon be in lots of trouble, anywhere but in an ideal kingdom. The trouble with reading Genesis 1 and reveling in our divine image is that most of us have read Genesis 2–3 and we know of our disobedience. The trouble with singing Psalm 8's description of our "dominion" over the planet in as positive a light as the psalmist is that we have learned how destructive human dominion can be. Is all of this simply too optimistic?

Bible-based Christianity must, of course, take seriously the reality of human sin. We have long since left paradise. No human government, neither David's nor any today, seems able to keep its early promises. Nevertheless, the story of David's early hope and the song of David's created glory remain Holy Scripture. We sing the psalm, and it becomes ours. Is hope warranted? Our texts suggest that it is, for at least three reasons:

1. Come what may, humans remain in the image of God. Israel knew full well the story of their expulsion from paradise, but they never quit singing Psalm 8. In some ways, Psalm 8 sings creation back into being, pushing back chaos and sin and claiming a new beginning in God's name.

2. Even in the midst of human frailty, God does new things in human history. The story of David's introduction is a perfect example. It takes place amid real historical ambiguity. The old king has failed and is on the way out. The new king may promise too much and is probably too young to be taken seriously. The implied conflict between David and Saul does not bode well for the healthy future of the nation. Still, according to our text, God is at work. God has chosen David, a human little lower than the heavenly beings, and will use him to exercise dominion over this particular moment in Israel's history. Despite appearances to the contrary, God is at work in the world.

3. In Christ, the true image of God (Colossians 1:15), we are restored and made new. Christ, who has the key of David, opens to us a new door that no one can shut (Revelation 3:7-8), and truly, once more, all things are possible.

CONSIDER OTHER VOICES

"Music has charms," wrote William Congreve, "to soothe the savage breast, / To soften rocks, or bend a knotted oak."

According to a recent study, students who listened to Mozart before an important examination got better grades. Native peoples everywhere understand the spirit-inducing power of music. Teenagers who crank up their stereos sometimes readily admit that it creates for them an escape, an alternative to present (but often not pleasant) reality.

In his case study of Martin A., Oliver Sacks, the physician made famous by the Robin Williams character in the movie *Awakenings,* reports that Martin could not live or pray without music. Though he was developmentally disabled and emotionally disturbed, "the marvel, the real marvel, was to see Martin when he was actually singing, or in communion with music—listening with an intentness that verged on rapture.... Martin was, in a word, transformed. All that was defective or pathological fell away, and one saw only absorption and animation, wholeness and health."[2]

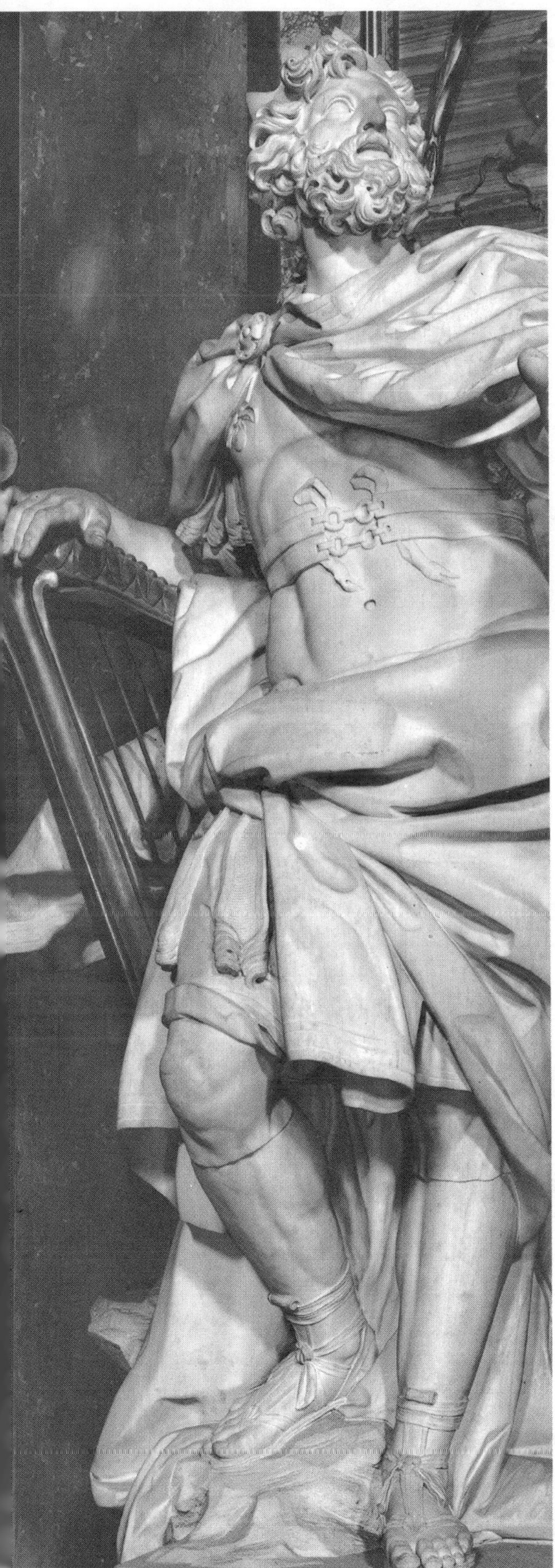

Statue of King David Pietro Pacilli (1716–?)

Throughout the biblical story, beginning with today's story, David is associated with music and the psalms. In the Apocrypha, we read a summary of David's life: "He sang praise with all his heart, and he loved his Maker. He placed singers before the altar, to make sweet melody with their voices. He gave beauty to the festivals, and arranged their times throughout the year, while they praised God's holy name, and the sanctuary resounded from early morning" (Sirach 47:8b-10).

What is it about music? About David and music? God and music? Healing and music?

On the other hand, Shakespeare recognizes that music's power is ambiguous: "Music oft hath such a charm / To make bad good, and good provoke to harm." Parents and police know the power of contemporary music for young people, but they are not always convinced that it is benign. Another of Oliver Sacks's patients, Mrs. O'C., is plagued by music (in her mind) that will never let her alone.

Now what is it about music? Is it good or bad? Is it of God or of Satan? How will we think about this?

BRING IT *together*

King David was a great musician. When he slept his harp hung from the wall over his bed. The winds are strong in Jerusalem. Each night the wind would blow through the strings of the harp and the harp would begin to sing. King David would wake and listen awhile to the music of his harp, and then spend the rest of the night studying Torah so he could be a strong and wise king.[3]

—Chaim Potak

MEANING & RESPONSE

WHAT DOES THIS MEAN?

Ours tends to be a cynical time. When surveyed, many people claim not to trust that the government or the business community or the media are telling them the truth. Conspiracy theories about national and world events often gain rapid acceptance. Political predictions and ecological predictions of the future are troubling. At a public level, hope is in short supply.

The David story, however, begins hopefully. David seems to offer so much promise. Israel's future looks so bright. Is hope warranted? Was it then? The Bible recognizes the human dimensions of the events that brought David to power. People are looking for leadership. David is a natural; Saul is weak. Even without God's involvement, the die seems to be cast for a Davidic takeover. But the biblical story claims that God is at work in the midst of this genuinely human drama. Can we believe that God is at work in the public events of our own time?

And what of us? Is there reason to hope? Can we see God at work in our lives?

During the troubled and dangerous days of the Reformation, when human power struggles raged everywhere, competent leadership was desperately needed by Christian congregations. But how could people know they were choosing wisely or well—especially when there was so little trust in the ecclesiastical system? Martin Luther wrote to such congregations:

> Let those who come together cast their ballots and elect one or as many as are needed of those who are capable. By prayer and the laying on of hands let them commend and certify these to the whole assembly, and recognize and honor them as lawful bishops and ministers of the Word, believing beyond a shadow of doubt that this has been done and accomplished by God.[4]

Luther's words were hopeful. Times were tough, decisions were difficult, choices were not crystal clear. Nevertheless, wrote Luther, trust that God is at work. God will not abandon God's world, no matter how hard the times.

And what of us? Is there reason to hope? Can we see God at work in our lives? In our leaders of church or state?

How will the David story help us think about these things? How can Christians be bearers of hope to a cynical age?

PLAN TO RESPOND

What difference would it make to the world if Christians talked and acted as though God were at work within it—both in the church and in the everyday affairs of business, politics, culture, and community life?

What difference would it make if Christian voices spoke of hope for the world rather than of cynicism and despair?

Christianity is not a "Pollyanna" religion. It does not look only at the bright side of things. But it does believe that the world is God's—the world as a whole and as it is. It believes that the world was made by God, has been redeemed by Jesus Christ, and is filled with the power of the Holy Spirit. It believes that the God who worked in the life of David, works in human lives today. What difference will this make?

In your thoughts and conversations this week—and also in your journal—try to keep track of how and why you interpret events positively or negatively. Remind yourself and others of the Christian assertion that God is at work, through the constructive efforts of human beings everywhere, to build up, sustain, correct, and guide us toward God's own vision of a just and blessed world. Take note of things within yourself and outside yourself that contribute to such a world and things that detract from it. At least daily, bring these thoughts to God in prayer, asking God to nurture constructive thoughts and actions and to remove destructive ones. Where possible, speak to others of your Christian hope, inviting them to join you in honest conversation about how we view the world in which we live.

WORSHIP

Catherine Cameron's hymn "God, Who Stretched the Spangled Heavens" looks forward hopefully to God's guidance in our lives. Sing or pray these stanzas, the first and third, together:

God, who stretched the spangled heavens
Infinite in time and place,
Flung the suns in burning radiance
Through the silent fields of space:
We, your children in your likeness,
Share inventive pow'rs with you:
Great Creator, still creating,
Show us what we yet may do.

As each far horizon beckons,
May it challenge us anew:
Children of creative purpose,
Serving others, hon'ring you.
May our dreams prove rich with promise;
Each endeavor well begun;
Great Creator, give us guidance
Till our goals and yours are one.

Catherine Cameron, b. 1927

1. "David" by D. M. Howard in *Anchor Bible Dictionary,* vol. 2 (New York: Doubleday, 1992), 48.
2. "Oliver Sacks, *The Man Who Mistook His Wife for a Hat* (New York: Harper & Row, 1987), 192.
3. Chaim Potok, *Davita's Harp* (New York: Knopf, 1985), 165.
4. "Concerning the Ministry" in *Luther's Works,* vol. 40 (Philadelphia: Fortress Press, 1958), 37.

Bridge

SESSION BRIDGE

LOOK BACK

- ☐ Although the biblical tradition comes to associate the entire book of Psalms with David, 73 of the 150 psalms are specifically titled psalms "of David" (Psalms 3–9; 11–32; 34–41; 51–65; 68–70; 86; 101; 103; 108–110; 122; 124; 131; 133 [though the term is omitted here in the RSV and NRSV]; 138–145). Consider reading 12 or 13 of these psalms in connection with each session in this unit as part of your study or devotions. This pace will take you through the list. You will gain a sense of the biblical editors' understanding of David's piety as they introduce you to these psalms associated with David's life and worship.
- ☐ If you desire additional information about Psalms, check with your pastor or church librarian about available introductions. These might include: J. Clinton McCann, Jr., *A Theological Introduction to the Psalms: The Psalms as Torah* (Nashville: Abingdon, 1993), or James L. Mays, *The Lord Reigns: A Theological Handbook to the Psalms* (Louisville: Westminster John Knox, 1994).
- ☐ The Bible reports to us the story and songs of David. Since he is a noted historical figure, you can also read more about him in histories of ancient Israel. A classic example is John Bright, *A History of Israel,* 3rd edition (Philadelphia: Westminster, 1981). Other valuable introductions include two books by Walter Brueggemann: *David's Truth in Israel's Imagination and Memory* (Minneapolis: Fortress, 1985) and *Power, Providence, and Personality: Biblical Insight into Life and Ministry* (Louisville: Westminster/John Knox, 1990).
- ☐ As you read and converse or pray and ponder about this course, keep at hand the Inspire Journal that is available for you. Journaling is an excellent way not only to record your thoughts and impressions, your experiences and feelings, your doubts and affirmations, your quiet prayers and joyful outbursts, but also to stimulate them. Writing encourages the creative process. You need not worry about style or structure or length or completeness, for no one will read this material but you—unless you choose to share passages with someone else.

LOOK AHEAD

- ☐ Prepare for the next session by reading 2 Samuel 5 and the related material in the participant book (PB, 15-24). Here we learn that David is made king of all Israel. He achieves remarkable political and military success. In Session 2, we will need to consider the source of David's success and how we think God works in political affairs.
- ☐ Also read Psalm 18, a psalm ascribed to David in thanks to God for his victories. It will, no doubt, raise significant questions for us: Is God present in human victories? Does God have enemies? How do New Testament Christians read these old texts?
- ☐ Other texts that will help prepare you for next week's study include Deuteronomy 6:1-15; Psalm 26; 1 Samuel 24:1-22; and Mark 10:35-45. As you read, keep track of your questions and responses in your journal.

Session TWO

the promise of SUCCESS

SESSION 2

2 Samuel 5:1-25; Psalm 18:1-50

EXPERIENCES & REFLECTIONS

FOCUS David is made king of all Israel and experiences military and political success. In this chapter of David's life, there is a purity that ascribes victory to God with a confident and thankful heart.

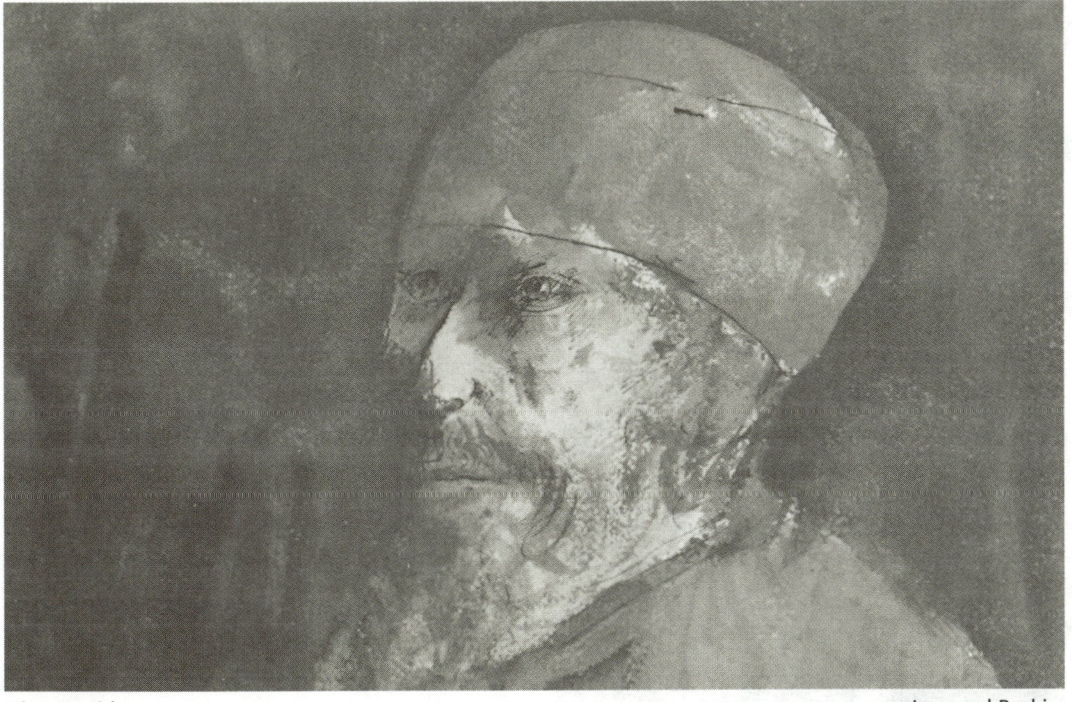

King David Leonard Baskin

Prayer

I love you, O Lord, my strength. The Lord is my rock, my fortress, and my deliverer, my God, my rock in whom I take refuge, my shield, and the horn of my salvation, my stronghold. For this I will extol you, O Lord, among the nations, and sing praises to your name. Amen.

NAME AND REFLECT

"Victory, victory, is our cry: V-I-C-T-O-R-Y!" David's mood in today's texts is a bit like our own cheers in moments of great personal and communal triumph. We might shout, with Robert Browning: "God's in his heaven—All's right with the world." (Some of us, of course, might think all was right with the world if that line occasionally read: "God's in *her* heaven!") Though perhaps fleeting, such moments are fun and invigorating. The adrenaline flows, the heart pumps, the emotions soar. When those feelings and those times are true and good, David is no doubt correct: the God who grants them is "worthy to be praised" (Psalm 18:3).

David's name in Hebrew, a detail from the above watercolor.

BRING IT *together*

God could be trusted, wrote David, because "the LORD is my rock" (Psalm 18:2). We still sometimes think of a friend or loved one as a "rock" of strength and trustworthiness. We speak of "living rock"—rock that is unbroken, still part of the earth itself, the kind of rock that provides a firm foundation for building.

Think in your mind of rock formations you have seen that inspire awe. Think of friends who are rocks—whom you can count on, come what may.

God is like that, sings David. Rejoice!

THE TEXT SPEAKS

START WITH THE BIBLE

The story of David is spread over many chapters and several books of the Bible. Our study can look at only a few passages. To fill in the blanks, you might like to read a relatively brief overview of David's life in a standard encyclopedia or Bible dictionary. If you would like assistance with this, check with your Inspire leader, pastor, or church or public librarian.

EXPLORE THE TEXT

Once again, our texts include both a narrative and a psalm. The texts are rather long, and there may not be time during the session to read them in their entirety. As you read in preparation, make notes of sections that raise questions and inspire particular insights, so that at least these areas can be brought up for discussion.

David Was 30 Years Old

David becomes king. Seven years here, thirty-three years there. Hebron and Judah, Jerusalem and all Israel. King of Israel, but too young to be President of the United States. These are the kinds of facts and figures that can give reading the Old Testament a bad name. "I started to read the Bible, but I got to all those lists and dates and genealogies and I got lost." Several people have made this point. So, what should we do? Produce a new "user-friendly" version of the Bible, with no dates, no places, no "boring" history, no irrelevant details? Maybe such a version would have its appeal, but it would be something less than the Bible. Does it matter that David reigned seven years and six months at Hebron, or that Jesus was born while Quirinius was governor of Syria? Only in two instances: (1) if we find ourselves on *Jeopardy* when the "Bible" category comes up, or (2) if we care whether or not the Bible is true! What all these facts and figures do is nail the biblical story down to real history. There was a Hebron, there was a Quirinius—maybe there was a David, maybe there was a Jesus. There is no "maybe," of course. David and Jesus are as well documented as any characters in ancient history. But without these "boring" facts and figures, that documentation would be impossible. The point is not so much to use the data to "prove" the Bible, but to recognize that the Bible is willing to make its case in the real world of history and politics, geography, and sociology. Rightly understood, these facts are not boring history; they are the detailed counterpart of the New Testament's claim that "the Word became flesh and lived among us" (John 1:14).

We live in space and time. Some of us were born in Ohio and studied in Germany and work in Minnesota; others were born in Mexico City, went to school in El Paso, and work in Los Angeles. The differences matter. They have to do with our "flesh," our existence in the earthly world that God created and loves. They make us interesting. All of us have family stories, passed on in oral tradition, maybe or maybe not verifiable by statistics and history; but all of us also have data that can be checked by the census bureau or the IRS. Both tell who we are. In the last session, we heard some family stories about David. Here we hear the census data. David shares the realities of our own lives, stories and facts, funny anecdotes and reportable data. Like us, David is a figure of this world, an historical person, a human being.

The City of David

In the United States we can think of Mount Vernon as the private home of George Washington or Monticello as the private estate of Thomas Jefferson, but we wouldn't think of Washington, D.C., as Washington's D.C. or Jefferson City, Missouri, as Jefferson's City. In the Bible, though, Jerusalem (or the oldest part of Jerusalem) was the "City of David"—David's own city. Conquered by David, it became, in some sense, his personal domain. Before Jerusalem was the capital of the United Kingdoms of Israel and Judah, it was the city of David—a fact that has great significance in biblical history. As neutral or Davidic property, Jerusalem more easily became the capital city of both Judah and Israel, precisely because it belonged to neither one. As the "City of David," Jerusalem came to be identified with the Messiah, the anointed one who was to come as the descendant of David and the legitimate king of all Israel.

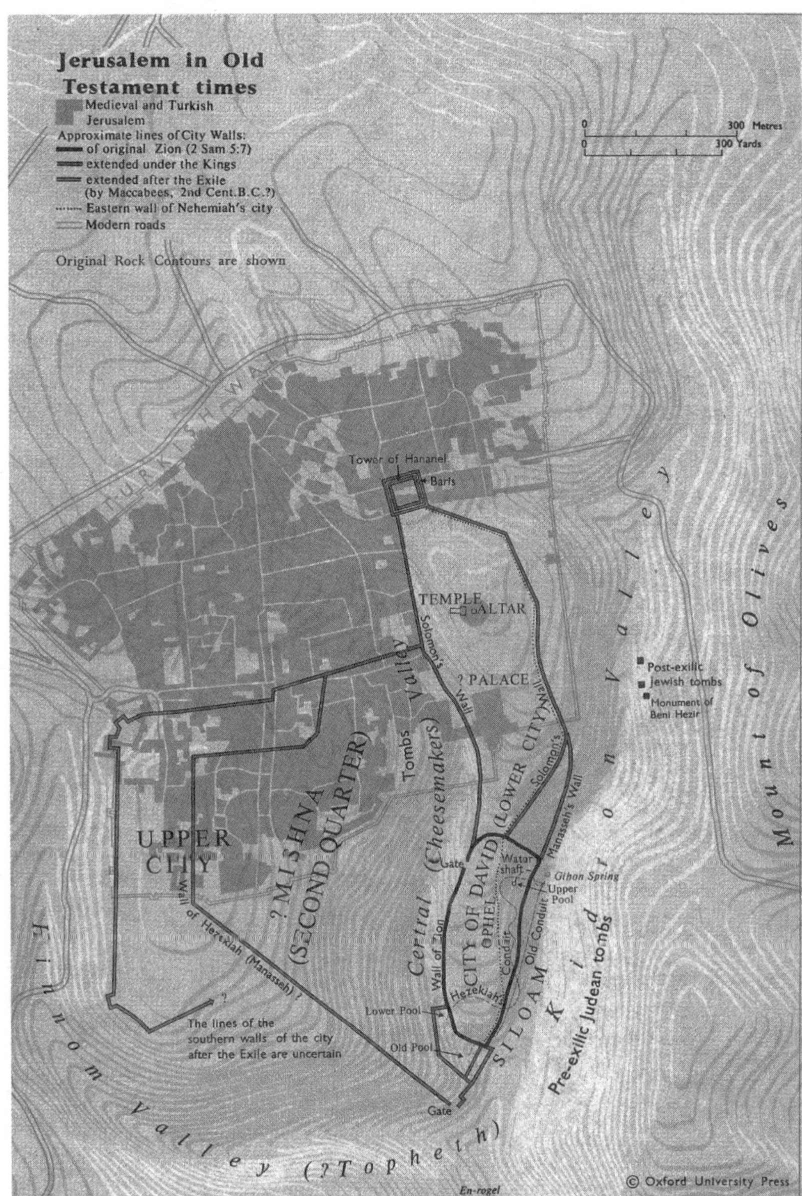

Jerusalem had been a Jebusite city, a stronghold of the Canaanite peoples who preceded Israel in the land of Palestine. It lay near the boundary between Judah in the south and Israel in the north. Its elevation made it an important stronghold. In other words, it was strategic property. David's capture of Jerusalem was a strategic move. The city became his, beholden neither to north or south. Naming it his capital made it more or less acceptable to both geographic areas. Identifying it as his own made him the legitimate ruler, not only of Israel but also of the Canaanite population that remained in Palestine. David was both charismatic ruler and political strategist. That combination is another example of the Bible's incarnational theology. Does God choose David to be his messianic leader? Yes. Does David conquer Israel to make himself political ruler? Yes. Politics and religion are not radically separated in the Old Testament world. Political reality and theological reality are never totally distinguished in biblical theology. God works in the world, and the world is a political place. If God's will is to be done "on earth as it is in heaven," this world, with all its political uncertainties, is the only place for it to be done. Biblical theology invites us to look for God at work in the real world—in, with, and under the political and geographical realities.

Politics and religion are not radically separated in the Old Testament world.

The New Testament teaches us that God calls people as his own out of every nation. This means that no one nation has the right to call itself the "people of God." On the other hand, wherever there are people of God, they will belong to real historical and political national groups. God will work within these groups or God will not work in this world at all. Politics and history are messy, but politics and history are the venues of an incarnational God. As biblical believers, we attempt to identify and name God's work in the only world we know, the world of the history books and the ballot boxes.

The Lord Had Established Him King

"David then perceived that the LORD had established him king over Israel, and that he had exalted his kingdom for the sake of his people Israel" (2 Samuel 5:12). Is this good news or bad news? Much of human experience would argue that people who think that their leadership is ordained by the gods (or by God) are the most dangerous of all. They can do no wrong. Whatever they do is the will of God. Their enemies are God's enemies, who deserve whatever fate is in store for them. Most of us are skeptical. We are not convinced that Henry VIII's murder of his wives was the will of God, divine right of kings or not. Most of us worry about any people's claims that its wars are "holy," ordained by God. On our best days, at least, most of us don't believe that God is either a died-in-the-wool Republican or a now-and-forever Democrat.

So what does the Bible mean when it claims that David's leadership was "ordained" by God? Three things, at least, are worth saying:

1. It was David who "perceived that the LORD had established him king." Easy for him to talk! Now, to be sure, the Bible as a whole claims that God was at work in and through David. David's perception is more than just megalomania. Still, David's perception will require third-party ratification—or third-party correction. The Bible never assumes that whatever David does is right, God's anointed king or not. God may work through David, and God does, but there will always be room for the voice of the prophet or the people proclaiming that the emperor has no clothes on. A biblical political theology always requires a balance between divine election and prophetic correction.

2. David's perception is shared by others. God is at work in the life of David, but God's work is not unrelated to the perception of the world held by others, others who may or may not share David's religious perspective. True, the most important thing about David's leadership in this chapter is God's choice of David, but there are other choices as well: first, the tribes of Israel recognize David's natural leadership qualities (2 Samuel 5:2); second, David's military cunning and prowess defy all odds, overcoming the initial negative perception of his chances by the Jebusites (the original inhabitants of Jerusalem) by entering the city in an unexpected way (verses 6-8); third, David's kingship is recognized by the surrounding nations (verse 11). Since God alone is God, God's choice of David is, no doubt, a free choice, accountable to God alone; still, David is one in whom others, too—believers and nonbelievers—recognize a special authority, a special power, a special presence. In this text, God works in the world, but not in a way that runs roughshod over the world's perception of reality. There may be times when God's ways are not the world's ways, but, in this text, God's ways are affirmed by the world. Here, God is deeply involved in human processes and human affairs.

3. The Lord exalted David's kingship" for the sake of his people Israel" (verse 12). This verse reverberates with the very center of biblical theology. God chooses individuals, to be sure—Abraham, Moses, David—but the choice, even of Jesus, is never to glorify the individual, it is for the sake of the people and the world. One possible attitude, for David or for any of us, is that God has given us a certain measure of leadership—in our families or communities or nations—so we might as well enjoy it and exploit it! Use it for all its worth! Another is the attitude of our text: God has given us leadership for the sake of others. The rules are altogether different now. Success is not measured by my fame or bank account, but by the prosperity of everyone with whom I come in contact, by my concern for the neighbor. Here, the standard judging David's leadership is the same as the standard judging Jesus' leadership: "You know that among the Gentiles those whom they recognize as their rulers lord it over them.... But it is not so among you; but whoever wishes to become great among you must be your servant, and whoever wishes to be first among you must be slave of all" (Mark 10:42-44).

My Rock and My Fortress

David used all his political know-how and military cunning to defeat his enemies and solidify his hold on the monarchy. Then, when it was done, he sang praises to God. "The LORD is my rock, my fortress, and my deliverer, my God, my rock in whom I take refuge, my shield, and the horn of my salvation, my stronghold" (Psalm 18:2). Can we trust his sincerity here, or is this just another strategy? We have, no doubt, all had moments when we wondered about the sincerity of particular political leaders as they ostentatiously invoked God in prayer and praise. Do they really mean it, or is it only a part of the script written by their campaign managers?

"The LORD is my rock, my fortress, and my deliverer, my God, my rock in whom I take refuge, my shield, and the horn of my salvation, my stronghold" (Psalm 18:2).

Psalm 18 is tied closely to David's life. Not only does the title link it with "the day when the LORD delivered him from the hand of all his enemies, and from the hand of Saul," (2 Samuel 22:1), the entire psalm appears as this chapter of 2 Samuel, directly drawn into the Bible's historical narrative of the life of David. Although the biblical writers are quite free in their criticism of David when justified, they clearly do not regard his praying this psalm as hypocritical. It is David's confession

David's response is one of faith, confessing his dependence upon God and singing God's praise.

of faith. David is well aware of the importance of human knowledge and strategy in governing a nation, but David also knows that a governance that feeds and nourishes, that frees and edifies, is the work of God. David's response is one of faith, confessing his dependence upon God and singing God's praise.

The images of Psalm 18 appear also in Psalm 46, where they became the inspiration for Martin Luther's hymn, "A Mighty Fortress Is Our God." The military images are disturbing to some: God as rock and fortress; "a sword and shield victorious."

> A mighty fortress is our God,
> A sword and shield victorious;
> He breaks the cruel oppressor's rod
> And wins salvation glorious.
>
> —Martin Luther, 1483–1546

"He trains my hands for war, so that my arms can bend a bow of bronze" (Psalm 18:34). Do we want to celebrate this view of God? A few words about this are in order:

1. The language assumes there are real enemies out there, real forces that oppress and kill, forces that oppose God's will in the world. Nothing in this imagery or in the Bible celebrates war itself, but it does celebrate God's protection against destructive powers. Most of us know places where it is not safe to walk. All of us, probably, have given thanks to God for getting home in one piece after experiencing danger. That is the sense of David's psalm, giving thanks for deliverance in the way one of us, perhaps a nurse, might thank a faithful police force for successfully protecting her or him on the streets they must walk to get to the hospital for the night shift.

2. Accordingly, the imagery of the psalm is overwhelmingly defensive. This is most often true throughout the Bible. Giving thanks that God is a "shield" and a "fortress" is not the same as celebrating God as a thermonuclear device. It is true that the Bible, too, seems to know moments when "the best defense is a good offense," and, truth to tell, there are some very difficult biblical texts in this regard; nevertheless, overall the Bible's military imagery serves to promise God's endangered people protection against oppression.

3. Though God can, for now, make use of military might, such images do not finally define the Bible's vision of God's goal for the world. The goal is peace. Thus, Psalm 18 closes with thanks for being delivered from violence (verse 48), and Psalm 46 sings praises because God "makes wars cease to the end of the earth" (verse 9). Finally, as that verse makes clear, there will be no place for any instruments of war, offensive or defensive, in the world God means for us. "God is love" (1 John 4:16) and "the LORD is a warrior" (Exodus 15:3) are both biblical statements, but, although the latter has its proper place in a dangerous world, it can never stand as a summary of biblical theology in the way that "God is love" can. Jesus comes as "Prince of Peace," a definition that will mark the hopes and efforts of Christians in ways that biblical images of warfare never properly can.

Reading the Signs

The description of God's appearance in Psalm 18 sounds a little like a modern insurance policy's definition of disasters as "acts of God." For the psalmist, God was like an earthquake (verse 7) or a volcano (verse 8) or a thunder and lightning storm (verses 11-14). In the ancient world, such overwhelming displays of the power of "nature" could only be caused by God (or the gods). Our insurance language is a remnant of the same thinking, and so are our folk wisdom and our mythical explanations (thunder, for example, as the sound of the gods bowling). We have scientific mechanisms these days that help us understand more clearly how nature works, but, in the moment of a flood or tornado or earthquake, we still stand in awe and we still resort to mythic and poetic descriptions.

Many myths and cultures have storm gods, rain gods, sun gods, or earth gods—and for good reason: the life-giving and life-taking powers of nature are awesome and quite beyond our control. The psalmist shares that worldview in part—surely God is in these amazing natural displays!—but only in part, for in the Bible God is one. There are not different deities in charge of terror and of compassion. The awesome God of the storms is the same God who loves and protects Israel, who promises to be with them always, who knows their names, who hears their laments and carries their burdens. In the poetry of Psalm 18, all this "natural" power comes in response to David's personal cry of distress (verse 6). The power is important, but not as important as the loving care with which God uses the power at his disposal. This is why God is worthy to be praised: he is a God not only of power, but of steadfast love (verses 49-50).

CONSIDER OTHER VOICES

Songs from Latin America

It is not only David and his warriors who sing God's praises for standing and fighting at their side against their enemies. Old Testament theologian Erhard Gerstenberger has collected songs from Latin American Christians that precisely echo the language of the biblical psalms. This one comes from Nicaragua:

> You go hand in hand with my people,
> you fight for them, in country and city.
> You line up in the worker's camp,
> to get your salary paid.
> You are eating there on the lawn with
> Eusebio,
> with Pancho and Juan Jose.
> You scratch your pan
> when there is too little honey in your
> food.[1]

This combination of God's solidarity with people in trouble and their shouts of praise in deliverance continues the themes of Psalm 18. Though it may claim that there are some who stand against God, it does not deny that God also stands with others (not only with "me"). It does not claim that God sides only with one people or one nation or one cause. But it does confess with the biblical psalms that, in this particular place and time, God stands with people in trouble and against injustice. In that sense, the biblical God is always "partisan."

The New Testament on "Enemies"

Although it would be a grave mistake to contrast an Old Testament "God of wrath" with a New Testament "God of love," it is always important for Christians to read the Old Testament in the light of the New. The New Testament is well aware that there are enemies of God and the gospel in the world, and that God's people will come under attack. Sometimes it echoes the language of the Old Testament, asking for God to judge these enemies.

Jesus, however, adds a new dimension when he says: "But I say to you that listen, Love your enemies, do good to those who hate you, bless those who curse you, pray for those who abuse you" (Luke 6:27-28).

In the midst of his painful death on the cross, he prays for his own tormenters: "Father, forgive them; for they do not know what they are doing" (Luke 23:34).

"Is he the God of the Old or the New Testament this morning?"

As New Testament Christians, we hear the call to love our enemies as a reminder, first, that God alone is judge.

As New Testament Christians, we hear the call to love our enemies as a reminder, first, that God alone is judge. Not only that, but God is a judge who loves those he is called upon to judge. We need not "affirm" the enemy to love the enemy. A prayer for God to transform the "enemy," to turn evil into good, to replace enmity with friendship, is always in order. So are honest laments, crying out to God in distress and anger, naming those who cause us pain. Still, even though the enemy may mean us genuine harm, as we are in Christ we recognize the image of God and the presence of Christ also in the enemy. At our best, we can resist what God resists, but we cannot hate those whom God loves.

Second, the call to love the enemy reminds us that the line between friend of God and enemy of God does not divide me from the neighbor, but divides me from myself. I, too, am enemy. In my sin, I become enemy of God and enemy of my neighbor. "I am my own worst enemy" is more than merely a cliché. To love the enemy is to recognize the enemy in myself and myself in the enemy and Christ in both of us. It is a cry for forgiveness and reconciliation.

BRING IT *together*

The bittersweet fruits of David's military success become clear in 1 Samuel 18:6-7: "The women came out of all the towns of Israel, singing and dancing, to meet King Saul, with tambourines, with songs of joy, and with musical instruments. And the women sang to one another as they made merry, 'Saul has killed his thousands, and David his ten thousands.'"

The women function here as cheerleaders. In their eyes, their song is altogether positive. But it cannot avoid reminding us that victory in battle for some means death for others and that success produces rivalries. David's story, like the rest of the Bible, takes place in a real and ambiguous world. One wonders: Does this world ever allow unmixed blessings? Can our songs of joy—no matter how wonderful—ever not hide a tear or two?

MEANING & RESPONSE

WHAT DOES THIS MEAN?

John Hercus is right. The point of our reading the David stories is neither to adore David nor, primarily at least, to learn history. The point is to ask what *God* is doing—in the life of David, in the life of the church, and in my life as well. That is the question that will make Scripture become Scripture for us—the Word of God that provokes and enlivens us.

> You see what I mean? These great and exciting days in the life of David are passed over in a flash. For the truth was then, as now, that the great task in the life of any [person]—David, or you, or me—is not the job we are doing for God but the job he is doing in us.[2]
>
> —John Hercus

PLAN TO RESPOND

Virtually everyone laments that they err on the side of not saying positive things to others often enough, rather than on the side of saying too much. In this session we have seen God at work in the life of David and attempted to name God's presence in our own lives as well. We can do that also for others. Make a conscious effort this week to point out triumphs in the lives of others—members of your family, friends, church members, coworkers, neighbors. Write some notes of thanks and congratulations, not only for good things done to you or on your behalf, but to people whom you see working for others or succeeding in positive ways. Include people of all ages; not just people in your age group. You may or may not specifically name these events as times when God has been present for these people or for you through them. If you can, it is certainly valuable to do that, but God works for good in us whether or not God's name is spoken directly.

You might consider doing this also as a group. Within your congregation or your community, identify people who are doing positive things or who have had personal triumphs and together send them a note. Perhaps you could explain that your interest was produced by Bible study, by learning to see God at work in the everyday events of life. These efforts will be productive. Others will feel better, and so will you. More, God will be praised.

Continue your journaling this week. Record your questions and insights as you read. Name for yourself times and places where you see God at work in yourself and others. History happens to us all, of course, but events become significant as we give them meaning. Attempt to do that for yourself in your journal.

WORSHIP

I call upon the LORD
  Who is worthy to be praised.
  So I shall be saved from
    my enemies.
The LORD lives!
  Blessed be my rock,
  and exalted be the God
    of my salvation.
For this I will extol you, O LORD,
  among the nations,
  and sing praises to your name.

—Psalm 18: 3, 46, 49

1. Antonio Reiser and Paul G. Schoenborn, *Sehnsucht nach dem Fest der freien Menschen* (Wuppertal: Jegenddienst, 1982), 36.
2. John Hercus, *David* (Chicago: Inter-Varsity Press, 1968), 39.

Bridge

SESSION BRIDGE

LOOK BACK

- ☐ In addition to the many nonfiction books and articles written about David, there are stories and novels as well. If you would like to read a novel as another way to fill in the cracks between the texts of this study, consider Malachi Martin, *King of Kings* (New York: Simon and Schuster, 1980). It is available in many libraries.
- ☐ Martin Luther wrote about finding ourselves in the psalms in his "Preface to the Psalter," in *Luther's Works,* vol. 35, E. Theodore Bachmann, ed. (Philadelphia: Muhlenberg, 1960), 253-257. You can find this volume in some public libraries, but your church library or pastor may also have a copy.
- ☐ If you started reading through the psalms of David, listed in this section of Session 1 (PB, 14), try to continue that process.

LOOK AHEAD

- ☐ As part of your preparation for the next session—and every session—pray for your own understanding and pray for the other members of your group. Try to do this individually and by name. Praying for one another will invite God's presence among you and for you and will link you together with a special bond.
- ☐ Read the material for Session 3 in the participant book (PB, 25-34) and the core texts: 2 Samuel 7 and Psalm 132. These are important passages. God's promise in 2 Samuel 7 (through Nathan the prophet) to build David a house is the basis for the Bible's view that the promised Messiah would come from the line of David. Psalm 132 includes the same promise. It might be called the "pulpit hymn" to accompany Nathan's sermon.
- ☐ Other biblical texts that will help you think about the next session include 2 Samuel 6; 1 Kings 8:14-21; Acts 15:13-18; Revelation 22:12-16. Record questions and insights in your journal.

Session THREE

the promise of A HOUSE

EXPERIENCES & REFLECTIONS

FOCUS David seeks to honor God by building him a "house"—a temple in Jerusalem. However, we are reminded that the future lies in God's hands, not ours.

Prayer at the Temple of Jerusalem James Jacques Joseph Tissot

SESSION 3

2 Samuel 7:1-29;

Psalm 132:1-18

NAME AND REFLECT

The Bible's wisdom teachers remind us that, finally, our affairs and the affairs of the world are guided by God:

The human mind may devise many plans, but it is the purpose of the Lord that will be established.

—Proverbs 19:21

The human mind plans the way, but the LORD directs the steps.

—Proverbs 16:9

Trust in the LORD with all your heart, and do not rely on your own insight. In all your ways acknowledge him, and he will make straight your paths."

—Proverbs 3:5-6

Prayer

We thank you, God, that you are a God of promise: you have given a land to Israel, a house to David, salvation to us and forgiveness of sins, your Holy Spirit to bring life and hope, and blessing for all people. Come to us in your promises, O God, and make us people of promise for all the world to see. We pray in Jesus' name. Amen.

Also look up Proverbs 16:1-2; 21:30-31. In these verses the Bible does not mean to say that God is some kind of blind fate, but it does want us to understand that God is God and we are not—and that is good news.

BRING IT *together*

David made God an offer. God made David a promise. A quotation by W. Bell in 1838 marks the difference: "An offerer is not bound until his offer is accepted. A promiser is bound as soon as the promise reaches the party to whom it is made."

Sometimes God makes offers, sometimes promises. Think of what difference this makes. Why is it important that the word to David in our text is a promise?

THE TEXT SPEAKS

START WITH THE BIBLE

Who will build a house for whom? That question, raised in 2 Samuel 7, needs to be read in the light of 2 Samuel 6. There David brought the Ark of the Covenant, the symbol of God's presence in Israel, to Jerusalem, his new capital city. The Ark was housed there in a tent, making Jerusalem the religious center of Israel as well as the political center. The political kingdom is symbolized by David's magnificent palace (2 Samuel 5:11). Would it not be only fitting that God should have an even more splendid "house" (2 Samuel 7:2)?

You shall not make for yourself an idol, whether in the form of anything that is in heaven above, or that is on the earth beneath, or that is in the water under the earth.

—Exodus 20:4

According to its title, Psalm 132 is not numbered among the psalms of David. Its content, however, is more closely related to David's life than most. It is the dramatic liturgy that tells in poetry the same story as the narrative in 2 Samuel 6–7.

EXPLORE THE TEXTS

A House for God?

Sometimes we speak of a church building as "the house of God." The ancient world thought of a temple in the same way, but they usually meant it much more literally than we. A temple was where a god lived, a roof and walls to protect and honor the idol that symbolized the presence of the deity. An ancient postal employee would have known immediately where to deliver a letter addressed to "God"; just look for the local temple!

It was only natural, therefore, that there would be a debate in Israel about the construction of a temple for Yahweh. Yahweh was not a God like other gods—obviously the Ten Commandments forbid making an idol or image to place in the holy of holies. Without an idol, why bother to build the building? God is loose and free. Still, some Israelites, like David, wanted to honor God and to mark Israel's place among the nations by constructing a great temple. What could be the harm in that?

Nathan's Yes—God's No

Initially, Nathan the prophet agreed with David about the temple (2 Samuel 7:3). We meet Nathan here for the first time. He seems to be something of a "house prophet" for David's court, turning up at significant places—here, to rebuke David for his sin with Bathsheba (2 Samuel 12:1-15), and as part of the palace intrigue that brought Solomon to the throne (1 Kings 1). Obviously his was an important voice at court. As we see in this story, he apparently played a dual role: he was both an advisor who spoke his own mind (2 Samuel 7:3) and a prophet, bound to speak the word of the Lord (7:4-17). This is an important distinction: Not every word from a prophet's mouth is inspired. A prophet's opinion (like any religious leader's opinion, then or now) has a legitimate place in the conversation; but it carries God's authority only when it faithfully conveys God's word. To Nathan's credit, he knew the difference.

Confronted by God, he moved away from his own conviction that a temple would be a good idea (or at least that pleasing the king would be a good idea) and challenged the king with God's counter-argument, that a movable tent is a more fitting symbol for Israel's God than an immovable house.

David's Choices—God's Choice

At one level, David's decision to bring the Ark to Jerusalem (2 Samuel 6) and his plan to build a temple comprised brilliant political strategy. Samuel and others had opposed the establishment of the monarchy for religious and practical reasons. Israel, they said, was not like the nations; it already had a king—Yahweh. Asking for an earthly king, in order to be like other nations, was a sign of little faith. Moreover, kings were inherently despotic; royal power would challenge Israel's concern, under God, for equality and justice (1 Samuel 8:4-21).

Bringing the Ark to Jerusalem no doubt helped David silence such objections. The Ark had been the symbol of God's presence since Sinai and throughout Israel's earliest history. David now used the Ark to identify his rule and his city with all the early traditions of tribal Yahwism.

The Ark, of necessity, was movable. It was the sign and the promise of God's guidance through the wilderness and into the promised land. Israel was a pilgrim people, on the move, going somewhere—both sociologically and theologically. The movable Ark was its fitting symbol. But a kingdom and a monarchy are fixtures of establishment. Their palaces and temples are strongholds, built on hill, masters of all they survey. They are going nowhere! A temple on a hill is the appropriate symbol for such a government.

David's decision to bring the Ark (the symbol of nomadic movement) to Jerusalem and "park" it on a hill (the symbol of permanence and power) seems brilliantly contrived to combine the old and the new, tribal tradition and royal hopes. David was no political beginner.

Surprisingly, though, given God's own objections to the monarchy and the temple, once these were established, they became identified—even by God—as God's "choice." Psalm 132 seems to "baptize" David's political strategies: "This is my resting place forever; here I will reside, for I have desired it" (verse 14). Should we read such a text with suspicion? Is it merely a hymn written by the establishment to co-opt God's seal of approval for what they wanted to do anyway? Kings and priests—like present leaders of church and state—are sometimes capable of such acts. But the psalms come to us as Scripture, the prayers of faithful Israel and the prayers of Jesus. We believe that God's "choice of Zion" is real, even if it did occur in and under David's political activity. As we have seen throughout this story, God moves and acts in the real world, compromised and ambiguous as it is. Happily, this suggests that God can and does work in the complex and ambiguous realities of our world, too. This never means that everything humans plan and do will be blessed by God; but God can and does choose to bless our work, even when our motives are mixed—good news, indeed, since we seem not to be capable of any other kind.

The narrative text of the books of Samuel remembers and reports the ambiguity behind Israel's decisions about the monarchy and the temple. The poetic texts, like Psalm 132, are more uniformly positive. The difference seems, in part at least, to be a matter of genre, of different types of literature. History and story are more likely to contain different points of view, to be more cautious; poetry is allowed to be more celebrative, grander, more enthusiastic. Similar differences can be found, for example, between the prose account of the crossing of sea (Exodus 14) and the poetic version (Exodus 15).

Noting these differences helps us read and think about how God works in the world. We rightly expect different things from prose and poetry. Sometimes at least, prose stays "down to earth," reporting the ambiguity of human affairs, while poetry soars closer to "heaven," rejoicing without question in what God is doing. Both are true, but they see events with different eyes and different purposes. The Bible's inclusion of both enlarges our vision.

Amid all the world's conditions and uncertainties, one thing is always true: God is for us.

Your Throne Shall Be Established Forever

If we try to read this story as though we have never read it before, we might well agree with Nathan: David's decision to build a temple is both reasonable and praiseworthy. Go for it, David! We, too, would want to honor God. We, too, might agree that it is not fitting for David's house to be bigger and better than God's. We, too, might want to "do something" to show our love and respect for God.

But the text surprises us, as the gospel always surprises us. Once again, the Bible makes its point: what we do for God is not the primary issue; the primary issue is what God does for us. David's resolve must make way for God's promise. God's promise will shape the future more than David's political strategies or religious commitments—significant as those might be. The "house" that matters ultimately will be built by God, not by David.

Our story makes clear in every chapter that what David does is significant. God works in this story in and through human beings. God's promise, the gospel, does not negate human history and human effort. But it does set human work in its place: human efforts will not establish the kingdom, God's promise will do that. Human effort, to be faithful, will work in response to and in accord with God's word. This story reports one of those moments when God seems to want to get our attention, to make us hear anew the ways of God. Amid all the world's conditions and uncertainties, one thing is always true: God is for us. God will not abandon us. "Right!" we say. "Yes! I knew that! *That's* the gospel: God's promise to us, not our work for God." We know it, but we always need to hear it again. The gospel is never something we learned once and, having learned it, have at our disposal. We always need to receive it as gift. It always comes as promise. It is always new.

"By God, for a minute there it suddenly all made sense!"

God's turning the tables on David changes the whole character of the story, especially if we contrast David's story with Saul's. Saul can be seen as one of the great tragic figures of antiquity. He is chosen by God for a great task, but, in the middle of his reign, he balks before one of the terrible decisions kings are required to make. As a result, God rejects him and chooses another. But the other, David, does not take office immediately. Saul's rule continues, even though we know it is doomed. No wonder he is depressed and angry. As characters in ancient dramas should, he dies fighting, finally at his own hand, going out both tragically and heroically.

David, too, has his weaknesses. His blessings, too, are mixed. But his story is not a classic tragedy, because he is not doomed to struggle against a seemingly capricious deity in the way Saul was. The change comes in this text. David's life will continue to have its ups and downs, but he need never again fear that God may cast him aside. He need never again wonder whether God will be for him or against him. He need never again fear to acknowledge his own weakness.

> The tragic hero is doomed by dark forces that are captured in the term 'fate.'[1]
> —W. Lee Humphreys

Saul's future was determined by God's rejection. David's future was guaranteed by God's promise. There is a world of difference!

The Unconditional Promise

The relation between David's plan and God's promise is strikingly portrayed in the language of Psalm 132. David "swore" to the Lord that he would build God a house (verses 2-5); but God "trumped" David's oath by taking one of his own. The Lord "swore" to David that a descendant of David would "sit on your throne" forever (verses 11-12). David had promised not to rest until he had fulfilled his oath (verses 3-4); but the psalm shows Israel (and us) that it is God's "rest" that provides assurance, not David's: God has chosen Zion as his "resting place forever" (verse 14).

Are you surprised that God should take on oath? This is not the only place that happens. By far the most frequent use of the term is in Deuteronomy (and deuteronomic theology elsewhere in the Bible) where God "swears" the land to Israel (for example, Exodus 13:5; Deuteronomy 7:8). In addition, God "swears" to keep his covenant with Israel (Deuteronomy 4:31) and, after the near sacrifice of Isaac, "swears" to bless and multiply the nation (Genesis 22:15-18). Whereas Abraham had experienced the terror of thinking God meant death for his son, God swears life to Israel forever. At moments of great crisis, Israel can trust in God because God has sworn to be faithful. Their confession of that confident faith is repeated often, using the same term for "faithfulness" that Psalm 132:11 translates as "sure oath": "The LORD, the LORD, a God merciful and gracious, slow to anger, and abounding in steadfast love and *faithfulness*" (Exodus 34:6).

God's promise to Israel is sure. God's faithfulness is forever. God's promise is unconditional. God's faithfulness is God's oath. Saul's terror of never knowing for sure whether God's rejection would push him aside is gone forever. The gospel, God's sure promise, wants to push aside our terror in the same way. Human religious experience often fears because it does not know for sure. Have I done enough to be good? If I die tonight, will I go to heaven? Do I believe the right things? Did I pick the right church? The gospel, whether here in the Old Testament or in the New Testament promises of Jesus, erases the terror: "And remember, I am with you always, to the end of the age" (Matthew 28:20). Of course, God cares, as do we, whether or not we are "good." We can and should work at defining our faith as well as possible. But there need be no fear in any of this. God has sworn an oath to us. In Abraham, in David, in Christ, we are God's own. God's oath is sure, and nothing can rescind it.

We can and should work at defining our faith as well as possible. But there need be no fear in any of this. God has sworn an oath to us. In Abraham, in David, in Christ, we are God's own. God's oath is sure, and nothing can rescind it.

The certainty of God's promise does not remove God's concern for justice and obedience. He says of Solomon, "I will be a father to him, and he shall be a son to me. When he commits iniquity, I will punish him with a rod such as mortals use, with blows inflicted by human beings. But I will not take my steadfast love from him, as I took it from Saul" (2 Samuel 7:14-15). In other words, Solomon will have to bear the consequences of his actions, receiving political or moral or physical blows from people as he delivers these to others—but nothing can separate Solomon from the love of God, just as nothing can separate a child from the love of a parent and just as nothing can separate us from the love of Christ.

God's own words imply that something is different now in God's commitment to David and to Israel. Once things were a bit more "iffy." Once God rejected his king. But no more. God is in this now for the long haul. God is bound to God's promise in a new way—just as God will be bound to people in a new way through Jesus Christ. God is not more "love" than he used to be, but God's love is more focused, more centered now in this commitment to David and Israel and later in Christ. This will be God's program in the world. God is pledged to it, and he won't go back on his word.

We have a picture of God's oath ceremony in Genesis, when God seals his promises to Abraham by passing between the severed halves of sacrificial animals (Genesis 15:7-21). God seems to be saying that he will break this promise on pain of death (see Jeremiah 34:18-19). Can God give his life for a promise? He did precisely that on the cross. That's how certain God's promises are!

> When the sun had gone down and it was dark, a smoking fire pot and a flaming torch passed between these pieces. On that day the LORD made a covenant with Abram, saying, "To your descendants I give this land."
>
> —Genesis 15:17-18

Satisfying the Poor

Why does God make an unconditional promise to David? Why does God choose Zion as his "resting place forever"? Psalm 132 provides an answer: "I will abundantly bless its provisions; I will satisfy its poor with bread. Its priests I will clothe with salvation, and its faithful will shout for joy" (verses 15-16).

God's work has a purpose. God does not turn David's resolve upside down just to show David who's in charge. God makes and keeps his promises because God is faithful, but God also works through his promises to achieve what God wants for the world: joy and salvation, blessing for all, and food for the poor.

The psalm assumes that God's acts have consequences, just as ours do. Suppose God wants people to be happy, to have what they need for meaningful life, to be free, to care for those in need. What should God do? One option would be to require it and to punish those who don't shape up. And, to be sure, God, like any parent, does command and expect certain behaviors. Still, it's hard to command joy and blessing. But God knows that setting people free will produce joy, that blessings will produce blessing, and so God is a liberator and a giver. The gospel, God's promise to be for us and with us, come what may, is good news. The psalm knows that it is also the best way to the good life. Both carrots and sticks produce results. Sometimes God will resort to both, but God clearly prefers the carrot. And, unlike the donkey, we even get to eat it!

Time to Rest

On the seventh day of creation, God rested (Genesis 2:2-3). God promised his people rest in the land (Deuteronomy 12:9-10). Now, at Jerusalem, God's rest and Israel's come together. God finds a "resting place" among his people (Psalm 132:8, 14). People can rest in the security of God's unconditional promise.

For Israel, the sabbath day was a time of rest. The Bible provides many reasons for this, but according to Deuteronomy: "Remember that you were a slave in the land of Egypt, and the LORD your God brought you out from there with a mighty hand and an outstretched arm; therefore the LORD your God commanded you to keep the sabbath day" (Deuteronomy 5:15). Israel rests because of God's deliverance. God's commitment, God's fidelity to his promise, sets Israel free to relax, to rest in the Lord. There are many things in the world worth working for. There are also reasons to rest. Sabbath rest for God's people is neither legalism nor laziness; it is a sign to the world that God provides—so fully, so completely, so faithfully, so graciously, that, for now, I can take a nap.

CONSIDER OTHER VOICES

God has done it all. We are free. Believing God's unconditional promise, what will we do?

We Sing

If the news is good, people sing. Sometimes they even dance. They cannot help themselves. If the tumor is benign, if you win the lottery, if the lost is found, if your sins are forgiven—you sing!

"Praise to you, O Christ"—This is the response to the gospel in *Lutheran Book of Worship*.

"Yakanaka vangeri"—This is the response to the gospel in the Evangelical Lutheran Church of Zimbabwe.

Our liturgical responses to the hearing of the gospel are formal reminders of spontaneous joy. In Africa, the spontaneity comes a bit more freely into the liturgy. People in Zimbabwe sing "Yakanaka vangeri" ("The gospel is good news") with great joy and a dancing step. Given good news, that dance is within us all.

We Satisfy the Poor

> If you believe, it is inevitable that nothing but good works will follow from faith. For just as faith brings salvation and eternal life, so it also brings good works and cannot be stopped from doing so.[3]

People worry sometimes that too strong an emphasis on the gospel—that God has done everything for us—will let us off the hook. People might not be motivated to do anything. The poor might not be fed, the neighbor might not be loved, the world might not be cared for. We need more stick! Luther makes clear that, where faith is real, such fears are groundless. We can stop good works among people of faith as little as we can command good trees not to bear fruit.

We Rest

O LORD, my heart is not lifted up,
my eyes are not raised too high;
I do not occupy myself with things
too great and too marvelous for me.
But I have calmed and quieted
my soul,
like a weaned child with its mother;
my soul is like the weaned child
that is with me.
O Israel, hope in the LORD
from this time on and forevermore.

—Psalm 131

There is a time to sing, there is a time to act, there is a time to rest. Psalm 131 (a song "of David") anticipates God's rest in Psalm 132 with calm and quiet hope. Here David—sometimes impetuous, sometimes warlike, sometimes ambitious—simply curls up with God like a child in a mother's lap. God allows that of us. Sometimes we can allow it of ourselves.

> The hope that God will find rest with his people bears perhaps even more eloquent witness to the God of the New Testament, for [the New Testament] speaks of [God] in the form of a servant. We see in fact something of the reason for his self-concealment, namely that the dwelling so far prepared for him [the temple] is not yet suitable and that his perfect coming to his own is still to be awaited.[2]
>
> —Gerhard von Rad

BRING IT *together*

In a sense, David wanted to play "you scratch my back and I'll scratch yours" with God. Or, to put a better construction on it, he wanted to do unto God as God had done unto him. David had a nice house, God should have one, too.

God, however, wanted to play "give-away"—as Native Americans sometimes do—honoring a special moment by giving things away with no thought of return.

- Name some occasions in everyday life when "you scratch my back and I'll scratch yours" is an appropriate way for us to play. Are there times for this attitude in the life of faith?
- Name some occasions in everyday life and in the life of faith when "give-away" is our best (or only) game.

MEANING & RESPONSE

WHAT DOES THIS MEAN?

How do we envision God? What kind of God do we want? The question is important because, as Martin Luther said in his explanation to the First Commandment in the Large Catechism, the God we believe in is the God we create for ourselves.

Do we want a God who turns the tables on us as God does with David in 2 Samuel 7? Or do we want a tamer god—one we could get on our side by doing the right things?

In his classic little book, *Your God Is Too Small,* J. B. Phillips lists several ways we might picture God, including, among others, "Resident Policeman," "Grand Old Man," "Meek-and-Mild," "Managing Director," and our own "Projected Image."

How are these images "too small"? What inadequate images might you add now to Phillips's 1954 list? Are some dangerous images particularly attractive to you? How might "too-small" images of God influence not only how we view God but also how we live, how we feel about ourselves, and how we respond to others?

PLAN TO RESPOND

We have seen that song, work, and rest are all appropriate responses to God's promises. Consider your own response first by reflecting on how you already sing and work and relax in faithful trust.

We sing in worship. Some of us "whistle a happy tune" at home. We skip and dance (more or less!) in response to good news. Remind yourself that this is a form of praise of God.

How do we "satisfy the poor with bread"? First, no doubt, through our everyday work. Obviously the farmer, the miller, the banker, the baker, the deliverer, the grocer—and a host of others—have a direct or indirect hand in providing bread for all. In one way or another, any honorable and honest work is used by God to provide for others. Think of how your own work—whether salaried or not—fits that role.

Rest, too, responds to God's goodness. It gives us life, it gives us time for self and others, it becomes an opportunity for meditation and worship.

We can also plan to use these avenues of response more fully. We might choose to sing for others by joining the church choir or helping with worship at a nursing home or another institution. We might build a house for others through Habitat for Humanity or feed the poor through Bread for the World. We might deliberately take time out from our own schedules to spend time with children or the elderly or the neighbor.

Join with others in your group in listing possible responses under headings of "Song," "Work," and "Rest." If some participants have similar interests, perhaps you can plan a group activity.

WORSHIP

God was present with David in Jerusalem before the building of a temple. We will be with God forever in the heavenly Jerusalem, even without a temple. God's promise is God's presence. Read Revelation 21:22-27.

We pray for Christ's presence with the second stanza of the hymn "Open Now Thy Gates of Beauty":

Gracious God, I come before thee;
Come thou also unto me;
Where we find thee and adore thee,
There a heav'n on earth must be.
To my heart, oh, enter thou,
Let it be thy temple now!

—Text: Benjamin Schmolck, 1672–1737; tr. Catherine Winkworth, 1829–1878, alt.

1. W. Lee Humphreys, *The Tragic Vision and the Hebrew Tradition* (Philadelphia: Fortress Press, 1985), 3.
2. Gerhard von Rad, *The Problem of the Hexateuch* (London: Oliver and Boyd, Ltd., 1966), 100.
3. E. Plass, compiler, *What Luther Says,* vol. 3 (St. Louis: Concordia, 1959), 1517.

Bridge

SESSION BRIDGE

LOOK BACK

- [ ] You may recall the 1985 Paramount feature film, *King David,* starring Richard Gere. Available on video, it offers another way to experience the broader story of David. Be warned, however, that it contains brief nudity and tends to embellish the story's violence, if only by portraying it in vivid color. It is not a film for children. Though often helpful, the movie is sometimes misleading in its inaccuracies. Viewing the video at home along with a few other members of the group could provoke interesting discussion. Why does it choose to depart from the biblical text where it does? What is lost thereby? What happens when a story is transferred to a different medium?
- [ ] If you would like to read more about the book of Psalms in a volume that is both instructive and devotional, look for Eugene H. Peterson, *Answering God: The Psalms as Tools for Prayer* (San Francisco: Harper & Row, 1989).

LOOK AHEAD

- [ ] Prepare for the next session by reading 2 Samuel 11, Psalm 51, and the material for Session 4 in the participant book (PB, 35-44).
- [ ] In the coming session we take a hard look at David's failures. In addition to the story of his adultery with Bathsheba, read also about his failure to punish his son Amnon, even for the rape of his sister (2 Samuel 13:21), and his inordinate mourning for his rebellious son Absalom (2 Samuel 18:33—19:8)
- [ ] The early church designated seven penitential psalms—psalms particularly appropriate for confession of sin. In addition to Psalm 51, these include Psalms 6; 32; 38; 102; 130; and 143. Reading these will give you an insight into the penitential piety of the Old Testament and a resource for your own prayer.
- [ ] As we read of transgression and repentance, we do so in light of the New Testament promise: "[God] has rescued us from the power of darkness and transferred us into the kingdom of his beloved Son, in whom we have redemption, the forgiveness of sins" (Colossians 1:13-14).
- [ ] Continue your journaling as you read and reflect on the meaning of these texts.

Session FOUR

a breach of PROMISE

SESSION 4

2 Samuel 11:1-27;

Psalm 51:1-19

EXPERIENCES & REFLECTIONS

FOCUS David's personal life reveals his—and our—human frailty and need for divine guidance and forgiveness.

David sees Bathsheba bathing and sends a messenger to fetch her.

Prayer

Have mercy on me, O God, according to your steadfast love. Wash me thoroughly from my iniquity and cleanse me from my sin. Create in me a clean heart, O God, and put a new and right spirit within me. O Lord, open my lips, and my mouth will declare your praise. Amen.

NAME AND REFLECT

Christian ethicist Werner Elert writes that adultery is more than a "breach of contract" or a "violation of the law," it destroys the "divinely fashioned existential situation."[1] In other words, adultery is not *grounds* for divorce, adultery *is* divorce—the act itself shatters the marital relationship. This does not mean that adultery cannot be forgiven, but it does mean that the marriage, like David's heart, needs to be re-created and renewed, at least where that is possible.

In our culture we speak of "broken" marriages and "broken" homes. Think of your own life or your own family or families you know. Where and how have "breaks" occurred? Have they been repairable? Why or why not?

Adultery and divorce are not pleasant topics for discussion. They are, however, very much a part of our lives. David's act and David's repentance might help us think about these things in biblical perspective.

BRING IT *together*

The refrain of the familiar gospel song is inviting:

> Come home, come home!
> You who are weary come home."
> Earnestly, tenderly, Jesus is calling,
> calling, "O sinner, come home!"
> —Will Thompson, 1847–1909

We embark on our study of David's failures and our consideration of our own in light of this invitation: Jesus' light is always on, the door is always open.

THE TEXT SPEAKS

START WITH THE BIBLE

We have made this point before, but it is worth making again: Do start with the Bible. Read the core texts and spend some time with them before reading the following material. Let the Bible have first crack at you. Think about what the texts mean on your own before you read the opinions of others. True, Bible reading is a communal business. We need the help of others. But we also need to allow the integrity of our own reading. Reading books about the Bible is like reading books about Plato. Almost all of them (at least the useful ones) are more difficult than the original. Yes, use the work of others; but, yes, trust your own careful and prayerful reading.

Psalm 51 is directly related to the David and Bathsheba story in 2 Samuel 11. This psalm is more closely related to David's life than most. That connection does not mean, however, that the psalm has not been prayed by countless other Jews and Christians. Linking the psalm to David does not deprive it of use by you and me. It simply tells us the gravity of the situations to which it may apply. It is available to those who commit adultery and murder—and also to those whose crimes are less but who feel equally separated from the love of God.

EXPLORE THE TEXTS

The View from the Roof

"It happened, late one afternoon, when David rose from his couch and was walking about on the roof of the king's house, that he saw from the roof a woman bathing" (2 Samuel 11:2).

Roofs are places of privilege. They provide access to scenes and lives that are meant to be private. They lead to temptation.

David's house was grand—the most magnificent in the kingdom. It already sat high on Mount Zion; so from his roof, his penthouse, David stood above everything and everyone. He was, he thought, the master of all he surveyed. It was a delusion, of course. Above him stood God, who had access to David's life and saw what he was doing when he thought he was alone. And God's knowing will matter deeply to the outcome of the story. Interestingly, because of the narrative, we, too, stand above David and see into his life. And that will matter, too. We will see David and ourselves differently because of our access to this story. It comes to us both as gift and as disturbing mirror, a way to see ourselves as others see us.

All of us probably have our own "roofs," places available to us but not to everyone, where we can see into the lives of others. Those may come from our jobs, our place in the family, our public life, or they may be quite accidental discoveries. We know things about others, especially about their vulnerabilities. David's abuse of his knowing reveals a temptation we all share. His story invites us to consider our own response to our rooftop views.

Taking What You Can Get

Having abused his privilege, David now abuses his power. He takes Bathsheba because he can.

He has learned immediately that Bathsheba is married. Her identity, "the wife of Uriah the Hittite," is made clear at the beginning and the end of the chapter (2 Samuel 11:3 and 26). This line serves, in fact, as a literary bookmark, showing the reader how the story of David and Bathsheba surrounds the story of David and Uriah. Each of the stories has two acts. In the first act of each, things seem fairly simple; in the second act they get more complicated *(see sidebar)*.

In Act 1, the David and Bathsheba story starts out as a mere dalliance, an afternoon's sport for a king who takes what he can get. Why not? Who will be hurt? But the act ends with the complication of Bathsheba's pregnancy, setting up the next story: David and Uriah.

In Act 1 of the second story, David seeks a simple solution to his problem. He tries to trick Uriah into thinking the child is his by giving him leave to go home and be with his wife. Uriah refuses special treatment, however—his integrity in sharp contrast to David's treachery—which sets up a new complication.

In Act 2, the David and Uriah story turns deadly. David's attempt to cover up his adultery now pushes him to murder. Treachery produces greater treachery; one sin leads to greater sin. The story mirrors life.

Act 2 of the David story, brief as it is, will produce its own complications. A child is born. What role will that child and a new wife play in David's already unsettled family? Who now will be the promised successor to David's throne? In bitter irony—or in a further attempt to avoid public scrutiny—David, who was willing to break the fundamental commandments against adultery and murder to gain what he wanted, now observes the lesser rule requiring a period of ritual mourning for Bathsheba. He honors formal convention to cover actual evil.

Is Bathsheba complicitous in the sin of adultery? She was the partner, after all. But in that world she had no choice. She was "sent for" and "gotten" by David. When Nathan uses a parable to confront David with his sin, Bathsheba becomes a "little ewe lamb" (2 Samuel 12:3), obviously unable to protest against being "taken" by the rich man. In this story, Bathsheba is a pawn. That does not mean she is of no consequence. God will make her the mother of kings, and she will come to stand tall in support of her own rights and those of Solomon, her second son (1 Kings 1:17-21). History, of course, will eventually find a fuller role for women; but for David, for now, Bathsheba was an object of pleasure.

A Story in Two Acts

ACT 1

A: David and Bathsheba (11:2-5)

B: Dealing with Uriah (11:6-13)

ACT 2

B': Dealing with Uriah (11:14-25)

A': David and Bathsheba (11:26-27)

The Child: Life or Death?

The final words of the story close one chapter and open another: "She became his wife, and bore him a son" (2 Samuel 11:27). Normally, this would be a time of great joy, especially given the promise in 2 Samuel 7 that David's offspring would sit on the throne forever. Indeed, the birth of a king's son produces the wonderful words of Isaiah, "For a child has been born for us, a son given to us" (Isaiah 9:6). But what about *this* child, this product of a sinful union?

The terrible truth is that the child will die, as Nathan the prophet informs David in the next chapter (2 Samuel 12:11-15). Unfortunately, this child, too, becomes an object—a sign of God's disfavor. The child will die as a consequence of David's violence. "You have struck down Uriah the Hittite with the sword.... Now therefore the sword shall never depart from your house" (2 Samuel 12:9-10). The point is not that the child is unloved or discounted, not by God and certainly not by David. David cares deeply for the child and pleads for his life despite the prophecy of his impending death (2 Samuel 12:16-17). David's prayer recognizes that God favors life and might even yet respond with grace. That God does not do so says nothing about God's concern for the child; it is a way for the story to make clear that the wages of sin is death, that acts have consequences, and that even kings cannot escape those terrible truths.

God will work through human affairs despite their inherent messiness.

This story does "use" a woman and a child to make important theological points to the reader. In that sense, it certainly reflects a time in history when women and children played, at best, secondary roles in public life. It is a story of its time, and could not be otherwise. The account would probably not bother us so much if it were not given theological interpretation. David committed adultery with Bathsheba. She became pregnant and bore a child, but the child died. Were that the story, we would accept it as a tragic and realistic account of the way things happen. But when we are told that the child dies because of David's sin, that "the LORD struck the child" (2 Samuel 12:15), we become uneasy. And perhaps we should. Breaking God's law brings uneasy consequences. The ancient world, seeing God more directly in the events of life, named God as the agent of David's punishment. We might not do that so quickly, but it remains true for us, too, that evil deeds produce terrible consequences—whether or not they are immediately visible.

God does not give up on David's family. God will work through human affairs despite their inherent messiness. David develops genuine love for Bathsheba, consoling her in her grief over the child's death. She conceives again and bears a son, Solomon, whom, we are told, "the LORD loved" (2 Samuel 12:24). Again, this does not mean the Lord did not love the first son; it certainly does not mean that Solomon will do no wrong; it does mean to tip off the reader to watch this child. God has important things in store for him.

A Sin against Whom?

Given the awful human results of David's arrogance—the abuse of Bathsheba, the murder of Uriah, the death of the child, the damage to the future of the country—it seems odd, disrespectful, and just plain wrong that David, in his prayer of repentance, cries out to God, "Against you, you alone, have I sinned" (Psalm 51:4). Doesn't this just further discount the human tragedy? Doesn't it once again turn the human characters into pawns?

In this case, the psalm itself makes clear that it does not mean to overlook the human dimensions of the story. The title remembers Bathsheba and that it was David's sinful exploitation of her that gave rise to his need for repentance. Again, the psalm wants to make a theological point: that all sin, no matter who else is hurt, is ultimately against God. In our day, we are more likely to speak of how violent and criminal acts harm human beings—which, of course, they do. The psalmist wants to say that sin hurts God as well, not to ask us to pity God, but to remind us that sin upsets the very heart and source of life, breaks the relationship with God that alone can restore us and those whom we have harmed to health and reconciliation. Psalm 51 makes the same point as Matthew 25:40: "Truly I tell you, just as you did it to one of the least of these who are members of my family, you did it to me."

Psalm 51's case becomes even stronger when we compare it with other psalms. Psalm 51 is an individual lament, sharing the features of many similar psalms. In these laments, the pray-er typically reports that problems arise because of his or her own acts, God's acts, and the acts of others. Psalm 51 radicalizes the proposal, however. There is no one for David to blame besides himself. The issue is his sin against God, pure and simple.

In that light, we have to regard David's prayer as a sign of maturity and health. He could certainly still try to pass the buck. "Mistakes were made," he might have said (as present politicians often do), because of the pressures of the office. He was enticed by Bathsheba's beauty (as modern rapists sometimes claim)—she should have known better than to bathe in the open. He need not play by the rules (as some celebrities seem to think) because he is, after all, not like the little people. He didn't ask to be a role model, so why should he be treated as one? David finally puts away all excuses. The fault is mine, he says, mine alone. I have sinned against God. Here he anticipates the words of the prodigal son: "Father, I have sinned against heaven and before you; I am no longer worthy to be called your son" (Luke 15:18-19).

"Father, I have sinned against heaven and before you; I am no longer worthy to be called your son" (Luke 15:18-19).

The Limits of Sacrifice

In ancient Israel, atoning for sin normally involved animal sacrifice. According to the Bible, this was not a human invention to appease an angry God, but the gift to humans of a gracious God: a way to overcome the terrible effects of sin. The Bible never clearly describes how this works. It is, no doubt, clothed in mystery. There is no purely logical explanation why the death of an animal should cover the penalty for human sin. It does make clear, though, that sin is a matter of life and death. Somehow, God accepts the death of an animal identified with the sinner as a reconciling act, a way for the sinner to be restored to God.

"Create in me a clean heart, O God, and put a new and right spirit within me" (Psalm 51:10).

Psalm 51, however, realizes that in this case no sacrifice will do: "If I were to give a burnt offering, you would not be pleased" (verse 16). The Old Testament never rejects sacrifice altogether, but it does recognize that easy sacrifice cannot mask gross or "high-handed" sin (see Numbers 15:27-31). If ever there was high-handed sin, it was David's sin in relation to Bathsheba and Uriah. This, clearly, is something no animal can fix—just as now it would be impossible to buy off God after adultery and murder with offerings to good causes or resolutions to do better. More is required!

The "more" for David was nothing other than re-creation. "Create in me a clean heart, O God, and put a new and right spirit within me" (Psalm 51:10). These words may be so familiar to some Christians from liturgical use that it becomes hard to hear their radicality. "Create in me a clean heart"—in other words, start over with me, God. Re-make me. The appeal is for sheer grace. I can fix myself now as little as I could have made myself in the beginning. Everything depends on your gracious renewal, God. Make me new—from scratch.

David realized that "the sacrifice acceptable to God is a broken spirit" (verse 17). Sometimes, this has been misunderstood, as though the human spirit or a human child must be "broken" in the same way that a bucking horse must be broken to the saddle. God does not want to saddle us, to tame us, to give us reins, but God does want to cleanse us from the arrogance that comes with being human, from the willingness to use another for our own pleasure or benefit, from the exercise of power to exploit rather than to set free. All of us, like David, are susceptible to that temptation. We pray, with David, to be freed from it, to be restored to the loving image of God.

The Possibility of Praise

What will David do if he is restored? According to Psalm 51, he will "teach" (verse 13), "sing" (verse 14), and "declare"—or preach (verse 15). As in the case of animal sacrifice, it would be possible to read this promise as some kind of "Let's make a deal" arrangement with God. Okay, God, you restore my life and I will repay you by bringing others into the fold. It's a win-win arrangement! I get to live, you get new converts.

Such a reading would be a monstrous caricature of biblical religion, however. David does not promise to preach and sing as a contractual obligation. He will sing and teach because he will. No one could not. "Which of you" having lost a sheep or a coin or a son and having found it again will not rejoice (Luke 15:4-24)? This is no obligation; it is simply true. Lord, restore me and I will sing—because restored people sing, restored people bear witness to others of their restoration, restored people bubble over—not because they should, but because they do. Restore me, O God, says David, and I will sing your praise, I will declare your word. We would, too, and we pray for the power to do it well.

CONSIDER OTHER VOICES

David's Children

In the language of the late twentieth century, we would have to admit that David's family was dysfunctional. Not only did he invite death and destruction through his sin with Bathsheba and Uriah, he failed miserably in the raising of his children. When David's son Amnon raped his own sister Tamar (following in his father's footsteps?), David "would not punish his son Amnon, because he loved him, for he was his firstborn" (2 Samuel 13:21). But what kind of "love" is this? It is at the same level as David's "love" for Bathsheba that took her because he wanted her. It is not a love that seeks the best for the other.

Similarly, David refused to respond appropriately to the treason of his son Absalom, coddling him rather than applying what we might call "tough love." When Absalom was killed—in a war of rebellion against his own father—David's inordinate mourning made it clear to those who had remained faithful to the king that they were "nothing"(2 Samuel 19:6).

Mary Louise Bringle

We can be aided in our understanding of David's grief over Absalom by the very helpful insights of Mary Louise Bringle in her book *Despair: Sickness or Sin?* Despair or depression can surely be a sickness, as it was for David—the debilitating reaction to overwhelming loss. But despair can also become sin, when we give in to it, use it to avoid difficult decisions, become useless to others, and refuse consolation. In its "very weakness," writes Bringle, despair "signals the distortion and enervation of a fallen will."[2] Without falling into the trap of blaming the victim, Bringle recognizes that, in separating us from God and neighbor, despair goes beyond illness and takes on the dimensions of sin. In his mourning over Absalom at the expense of his faithful followers, David gave in to the sin of despair.

David and Jonathan meet. Not all David's human relationships were flawed. His love for his friend Jonathan, Saul's son, never diminished.

M. Scott Peck

Another contemporary writer who recognizes that psychological dysfunction can have evil (not just clinical) results is M. Scott Peck in his book *People of the Lie: The Hope for Healing Human Evil*. From Peck's psychological perspective, evil is "the use of power to destroy the spiritual growth of others for the purpose of defending and preserving the integrity of our own sick selves."[3] Again, David is guilty. He uses power to destroy Bathsheba and Uriah for the sake of his own sick desires. As Peck recognizes in his own clinical practice, such actions are not merely illness, they are evil.

BRING IT *together*

David was guilty of murder and adultery. Some of us are too. And the comfort of Psalm 51, with its promise of re-creation and renewal, will be powerful. But in the Sermon on the Mount, Jesus reminds us that whoever hates or whoever lusts is already guilty of murder and adultery (Matthew 5:21-22, 27-28). They have already alienated themselves from the neighbor and from God. In that sense, the story of David's sin and David's confession applies to us all. Like David, we seek a new heart and a new spirit.

MEANING & RESPONSE

WHAT DOES THIS MEAN?

The Lord sent the prophet Nathan to David to answer the question "What does this mean?" Once there was a very rich man, said Nathan, who had more sheep than he could count. Nearby lived a very poor man with one little ewe lamb—a pet that lived in his house and shared his life. It was like a daughter to him. But when the rich man needed a lamb to make dinner for a visitor, he took the poor man's only lamb rather than one of his thousands.

Terrible! said David. Evil! This man deserves to die. Nathan said to David, "You are the man!"

The task of the prophet or the preacher is to catch the attention of a particular person or group so they hear that the biblical message—both promises and accusations—is for them. As we listen to the Bible, we are the woman, we are the man to whom it speaks.

In the Gospel of Matthew, Jesus institutes the Lord's Supper and immediately afterward, predicts Peter's denial of Christ. Soon after, Jesus is led to the cross. Both David's story of betrayal against his neighbors and God, and Peter's denial of the one he confesses to be God confront us with our own sin, our own denials, our own betrayals against neighbor and God.

> Then Jesus said to them, "You will all become deserters because of me this night; for it is written, 'I will strike the shepherd, and the sheep of the flock will be scattered.'
> But after I am raised up, I will go ahead of you to Galilee." Peter said to him, "Though all become deserters because of you, I will never desert you." Jesus said to him, 'Truly I tell you, this very night, before the cock crows, you will deny me three times." Peter said to him, "Even though I must die with you, I will not deny you." And so said all the disciples.
>
> —Matthew 26:31-35

PLAN TO RESPOND

As king, David was able to get away with murder. Well, not finally. God knew. But David was never brought before an earthly court. Most people caught in murder or other crimes must pay a civil penalty. Without condoning crime, Psalm 51 reminds us that there is no criminal in whom God will refuse to create a new heart in response to faithful repentance. Criminals, too, need the assurance of God's love; they, too, are neighbors to be served. Many church groups offer various kinds of outreach ministry to prisoners. Perhaps you or your group would like to participate. Your local council of churches or synod or denominational office should be able to provide your with information.

WORSHIP

In Christ we are made new. We go, therefore, "on our way rejoicing." Pray or sing together the following hymn:

On our way rejoicing
Gladly let us go.
Christ our Lord has conquered;
Vanquished is the foe.
Christ without, our safety;
Christ within, our joy;
Who, if we be faithful,
Can our hope destroy?
On our way rejoicing;
As we forward move,
Hearken to our praises,
O blest God of love!

—John S. B. Monsell, 1811– 1875, alt.

---

1. Werner Elert, *The Christian Ethos* (Philadelphia: Muhlenberg Press, 1957), 90.
2. Mary Louise Bringle, *Despair: Sickness or Sin?* (Nashville: Abingdon Press, 1990), 148.
3. M. Scott Peck, *People of the Lie: The Hope for Healing Human Evil* (New York: Simon and Schuster, 1983), 119.

SESSION BRIDGE

LOOK BACK

- [ ] Two Christian writers of the twentieth century can help us in our meditation on the Psalms. Look for C. S. Lewis, *Reflections on the Psalms* (London: Geoffrey Bles, 1958) and Martin Marty, *A Cry of Absence* (San Francisco: Harper and Row, 1983).
- [ ] If you did not read the whole terrible story of Amnon and Tamar in preparation for this session, consider doing so now (2 Samuel 13:1-22). Brutal in its honesty, it is one of those stories that saddens us by its presence while, at the same time, encourages us about the integrity of the biblical writers. They were quite willing to tell the unvarnished truth about biblical characters.
- [ ] Try to continue with your allotted reading of the psalms of David (PB, 14). Make use of your journal as much as possible. You will discover that written interaction with what you read enhances the reading itself and also your memory of it.

LOOK AHEAD

- [ ] Prepare for the next session by reading the material in the participant book (PB, 45-54) and the core texts: 1 Samuel 17 and Psalm 23. At significant moments in David's life, he is identified as a shepherd. We will examine the shepherd image when we next meet. Use the worksheet you will receive at the end of this session to prepare for the study of Psalm 23 next time.
- [ ] Look at psalms that depict God as shepherd (in addition to Psalm 23) such as Psalms 80 and 100. Significantly, both God and David are seen as shepherd in Psalm 78 (verses 52-53, 70-72).
- [ ] Read other important shepherd passages in the Bible (for example, Ezekiel 34:1-31; John 10:1-18; Hebrews 13:20-21; Revelation 7:13-17.

Session FIVE

the promised SHEPHERD

EXPERIENCES & REFLECTIONS

SESSION 5

1 Samuel 17:1-58; Psalm 23:1-6

FOCUS The dangers David meets as a shepherd prepare him for combat with Goliath, the "giant" of the Philistines. Shepherd images play an important role in the life of David. They set the stage for the New Testament's introduction of Jesus as the Good Shepherd.

Tanja Butler

Prayer

The LORD is my shepherd, I shall not want. He makes me lie down in green pastures; he leads me beside still waters; he restores my soul. He leads me in right paths for his name's sake. Even though I walk through the darkest valley, I fear no evil; for you are with me; your rod and your staff—they comfort me. You prepare a table before me in the presence of my enemies; you anoint my head with oil; my cup overflows. Surely goodness and mercy shall follow me all the days of my life, and I shall dwell in the house of the LORD my whole life long. Amen (Psalm 23:1-6).

NAME AND REFLECT

Remember our reading of Psalm 8 in Session 1? According to that psalm—a psalm attributed to David—one of the signs that human beings were created in the image of God, "a little lower than the angels," was their ability to domesticate animals: "You have given them dominion over the works of your hands; you have put all things under their feet, all sheep and oxen, and also the beasts of the field, the birds of the air, and the fish of the sea, whatever passes along the paths of the seas" (Psalm 8:6-8).

Domestication of animals is one of the earliest examples of human "technology." How responsibly have we exercised this God-given "dominion"? The role of the human in creation, both positive and negative, parallels the role of David as shepherd of Israel. Both he and we sometimes get it right, to the glory of God; but sometimes he and we do not. The Bible tells David's story and ours with remarkable candor.

BRING IT *together*

All of us have seen pictures of Jesus as the Good Shepherd. The artist means to provide an image of comfort and trust. We are lambs in God's own arms.

Does the picture work for you? Some will find it nostalgic and warm. Others may have rarely seen a sheep, much less a shepherd. What images of God provide comfort for you?

THE TEXT SPEAKS

START WITH THE BIBLE

Today's narrative moves back to the beginnings of the David story. Don't be confused by our shifting chronology. We are not preparing for an objective quiz on the life of David (though accurate biblical knowledge can't hurt!) so much as gleaning material from David's story to nourish our own life of faith. One of the important features of the David story is the use of shepherd imagery. That is our focus in this session, both in the narrative of 1 Samuel 17 and the poetry of Psalm 23.

EXPLORE THE TEXTS

Feeding His Father's Sheep

When we (along with Samuel) first met David, he had to be summoned from the field where he was keeping the sheep (1 Samuel 16:11). When Saul needed help in his depression, David was summoned again—and again from among the sheep (1 Samuel 16:19). Now the Philistines are advancing in renewed threat; and, once more, we are going to need David. But "where is the boy who looks after the sheep?" Where he belongs, of course—though, unlike the boy in the nursery rhyme, David is not under a haystack fast asleep. He is the faithful and watchful shepherd, ever diligent to make sure the sheep are secure (1 Samuel 17:15, 20).

At significant points, the narrator uses the image of shepherd to describe David. In these early texts the picture seems to serve a dual purpose: On the one hand, it reminds us that David is young, that not much is expected of him. In tribal cultures, it is still often the young children who are sent out to care for the sheep and goats. On the other hand, we, like the original hearers of this story, know that shepherding has other connotations in the Bible. The king is a shepherd (2 Samuel 5:2); and so is God (Psalm 80:1)! Gods and leaders were depicted as shepherds throughout the ancient Near East.

The biblical narrator uses this multipurpose image to capture our attention and imagination. David, from the beginning, is the shepherd boy; but we hear the word play and know he is also to be the shepherd king. We will be eager to see how this young upstart will deal with the responsibilities thrust upon him.

Lions and Giants and Bears

For 40 days running, Israel's army is taunted by Goliath, the great champion of the Philistines. The biblical story of David and Goliath has all the elements of a John Wayne movie—or of a classic fairy tale: the huge and evil bully, the frightened masses, the pure and unexpected hero, the snickering of his comrades and the disdain of the enemy, the miraculous triumph of good, nobility and the king's daughter as a reward. Indeed, the story may have been exaggerated in the telling throughout the generations. Elsewhere the Bible recalls that Goliath was defeated by someone named Elhanan (2 Samuel 21:19). Might the story have been "transferred" to David as a way of enhancing him as the Israelite leader par excellence? Or as a way to say that all of God's victories have a certain Davidic or messianic quality? At this juncture we cannot be sure—though we are sure that even in the story as it stands the primary point is not the figure of David, or of Elhanan, but trust in the deliverance of God who "does not save by sword and spear" (1 Samuel 17:45-47). The story makes us see this by having David removes Saul's armor before the battle (verses 38-40). The victory is God's, and everyone on the set, in the whole cast of thousands, must understand this (verse 47).

According to the Hebrew text, Goliath was 9 feet, 9 inches tall—a giant even in the NBA! The Greek version may be more accurate; it measures him in at 6 feet, 9 inches—already a "giant" by the standards of the ancient world. He would have required gigantic strength to wear a 125-pound coat of mail and wield a 15-pound spear! The spearhead was iron, a metal that was harder than bronze and relatively new to the region of Palestine. Access to iron technology was apparently jealously guarded by the Philistines (1 Samuel 13:19-22). The biblical interest in iron and its secrets reminds us that our story takes place toward the beginning of the iron age in that part of the world.

Here, again, David's shepherd role works in a twofold way. David is the shepherd boy, a mere lad, fit only to care for the sheep or serve as an errand boy for the "real" soldiers (1 Samuel 17:17-18). But, as fate (or God!) would have it, it is precisely the shepherd stuff in his résumé that prepares him for the battle to come. Guarding the flock required him to take on "both lions and bears"—single-handedly and bare-handed! His confidence and his confession are sure: "The LORD, who saved me from the paw of the lion and from the paw of the bear, will save me from the hand of this Philistine" (verse 37).

David was willing to stand up to lions and bears in order to rescue a single lamb (verses 34-35). Once more, we see a foreshadowing here of the biblical picture of the Good Shepherd. The young David has paved the way for all that is to come.

The LORD, who saved me from the paw of the lion and from the paw of the bear, will save me from the hand of this Philistine.

1 Samuel 17:37

Playing by the Rules

Goliath's challenge calls for Israel to send its champion against him, the champion of the Philistines, and to have both armies agree to abide by the outcome of this one-on-one combat. This seems odd to those of us steeped in modern notions of "total war." Who would agree to such a thing? Fine, give it a shot—but if we lose, we'll still come at you with rockets, grenades, and nukes, if necessary. Perhaps the ancients were more civilized. War, though always terrible, still retained a certain ritualized or stylized quality. As in chess, there were rules to be obeyed. Commentators find parallels in Greek and Egyptian literature where, too, armies agree to honor the outcome of a battle between two warriors. The practice of counting coup by North American Plains Indians may have had a similar ritualistic character: it was apparently more courageous to ride in and touch an enemy (showing one *could* have killed him) than actually to use a weapon. Bravery and superiority are established, but fewer people die.

As our story shows, finally people then and now are not so different. According to the contract, David's victory over Goliath should have put an end to the matter, but it precipitates a complete and bloody rout of the Philistine forces by the Israelite army (verses 51-53). Perhaps it was the Philistine panic (verse 51) that incited the Israelite chase. At any rate, war becomes as hellish then as it does in every age. Limits, even when agreed upon, are hard to maintain.

Shepherd of My People Israel

Years later, when at last David succeeds to the throne of Israel, the shepherd image returns. In the intervening period, David has been an outlaw, a fugitive, and a warrior; but now God says, "It is you who shall be shepherd of my people Israel" (2 Samuel 5:2). Again, when God promises to build David a house, the text plays with the two meanings of *shepherd:* God takes David "from the pasture" to take his place among the tribal leaders whom God commanded "to shepherd" the people (2 Samuel 7:7-8). The narrator and God keep reminding David and us of his shepherd role.

There is, no doubt, a certain measure of irony in this. The Bible knows that good leaders are to be like good shepherds; but it also knows that kings and shepherds have great power and that such power that can be massively abused. When the people first ask for a king, Samuel reminds them of the "ways of the king": among other things, "he will take one-tenth of your flocks, and you shall be his slaves" (1 Samuel 8:11-18). The shepherd becomes the sheep-stealer.

The prophets, especially Jeremiah and Ezekiel, condemn the false shepherds who scatter the flock of Israel. "You eat the fat, you clothe yourselves with the wool, you slaughter the fatlings; but you do not feed the sheep" (Ezekiel 34:3; see Jeremiah 23:1-2).

The solution to the problem of bad shepherds, for both Jeremiah and Ezekiel, is the return of a shepherd in the image of David, a good and righteous leader: "I will set up over them one shepherd, my servant David, and he shall feed them: he shall feed them and be their shepherd. And I, the LORD, will be their God, and my servant David shall be prince among them; I, the LORD, have spoken" (Ezekiel 34:23-24; see Jeremiah 23:4-5). Again, David becomes the ideal shepherd, the pure, heroic shepherd boy who becomes the good and righteous king.

But every reader of the Bible, along with David himself, knows that something rings false here. David has not always lived up to the promise, and the sheep have suffered. God may raise up a Good Shepherd in the image of David, but that will show God's grace more than David's perfection. Toward the end of his life, when David's failure yet once again brings death and destruction to his people, the king offers this poignant prayer: "I alone have sinned, and I alone have done wickedly; but these sheep, what have they done?" (2 Samuel 24:17).

Tending the Ewes

David's greatest failure, of course, was his adulterous seizure of Bathsheba and subsequent murder of her husband Uriah. Here, too, the Bible uses the shepherd image to devastating effect.

According to Psalm 78:70-71, God "chose his servant David, and took him from the sheepfolds; from tending the nursing ewes he brought him to be the shepherd of his people Jacob." And, as we have seen, as a lad David did offer his own life for the sake of the lambs. Thus, the irony of Nathan's parable in response to David's wickedness is all the more bitter: "The rich man had very many flocks and herds; but the poor man had nothing but one little ewe lamb" (2 Samuel 12:2-3). David has gone from tending the ewes to seducing them, from feeding them to abusing them, from protecting them to becoming their enemy.

God himself continues to demonstrate the proper relationship between power and compassion. God's power brings liberation, not servitude. God's strong arm is the same arm of compassion that gathers the tender lambs.

See, the Lord God comes with might,
 and his arm rules for him;
his reward is with him,
 and his recompense before him.
He will feed his flock like a shepherd;
 he will gather the lambs in his arms,
and carry them in his bosom,
 and gently lead the mother sheep.
—Isaiah 40:10-11

David and we are chastened by such biblical pictures. Humans fail in their shepherding, even David, but God continues to use the shepherd image to portray the proper care of humans for one another. God will use the promise he saw and invested in David, despite David's failures. God may even do the same with us!

The Lord Is My Shepherd

The best known of David's psalms helps us bridge the gap between failure and promise. How will David recapture his potential as shepherd? Not, evidently, by relying on his own resolve or his own job description, but by remembering that even though he is shepherd of Israel, he, too, is shepherded: "The LORD is my shepherd, I shall not want" (Psalm 23:1).

Psalm 23 is a simple, yet profound, psalm of trust. Form critics point out that psalms of trust are related to individual lament psalms, which often contain brief confessions of trust within their outbursts of alienation and distress. In other words, the deep trust of Psalm 23 is not unfamiliar with pain. There is no hint or promise of a "carefree" life for one of God's flock. In the midst of turmoil, however, trust and hope are given or received or discovered. The pray-er, like David, trusts nevertheless. Despite his own failures, despite his dysfunctional family, despite succumbing to Samuel's prediction that a king would fleece the flock, David now remembers the true shepherd—and in that remembering he becomes again a faithful shepherd of Israel.

Psalm 23 can be divided and understood in more than one way. Many have pointed out that it contains two primary images: the psalmist as God's carefully protected sheep (verses 1-4) and as a participant in a temple thankoffering meal (verses 5-6). The two halves of the psalm are closely connected, however, in an ABB'A' structure.

Psalm 23

A	God as "Lord"	guidance	23:1-3
B	God as "you"	presence	23:4
B'	God as "you"	presence	23:5
A'	God as "Lord"	guidance	23:6

Trust derives from knowing that I can address the "Lord," the God of Israel, as "you." The God who guides and protects me is the God who is with me and who feeds me. With this God I can surely live forever.

The Good Shepherd

Knowing David's story, we may be surprised at how glowingly biblical tradition remembers him. He was, to be sure, a heroic figure, and the intertestamental book of Sirach celebrates the young shepherd in heroic terms: "He played with lions as though they were young goats, and with bears as though they were lambs of the flock. In his youth did he not kill a giant, and take away the people's disgrace?" (Sirach 47:3-4).

> What is it that makes David endlessly fascinating to us? Why is it that the tradition has not lingered over Saul or Solomon or anyone else the way it has lingered over David?
>
> I propose to think this way. On the one hand, David is much like us. There is something genuinely human about him, which means that there is a shape to his life that we can count on and identify with.... But even while we are able to identify with him, there is distance between David and us. That distance is because of his nerve and grandeur in which he can make the great gesture that carries everyone before him.... There is, then, the ability to identify with and yet to be called out beyond ourselves, for we know we are in the presence of greatness.[2]
>
> —Walter Brueggemann

Following the destruction of Jerusalem, David's city, Psalm 89 still remembers the glories of old:

> Then you spoke in a vision to your faithful one, and said:
> "I have set the crown on one who is mighty,
> I have exalted one chosen from the people.
> I have found my servant David;
> with my holy oil I have anointed him;
> My hand shall always remain with him;
> my arm also shall strengthen him.
>
> —Psalm 89:19-21

But the psalmist also remembers that David's glory was never his own doing:

> My faithfulness and steadfast love shall be with him;
> and in my name his horn shall be exalted....
> He shall cry to me, "You are my Father,
> my God, and the Rock of my salvation!"
> I will make him the firstborn,
> the highest of the kings of the earth.
> Forever I will keep my steadfast love for him,
> and my covenant with him will stand firm.
>
> —Psalm 89:24-28

But, where do we go from here, the psalmist wonders, now that David's splendor is in ruins.

> But now you have spurned and rejected him;
> you are full of wrath against your anointed....
> Lord, where is your steadfast love of old,
> which by your faithfulness you swore to David?
>
> —Psalm 89:38, 49

It seems clear that the way back, the path to renewal, can only come from a new act of love and mercy by God himself. No matter how heroic, human efforts were insufficient to maintain the kingdom.

Ezekiel understands that a new kingdom will be possible only when God himself becomes "the shepherd of my people."

> I will feed them with the good pasture.... there they shall lie down in good grazing land, and they shall feed on rich pasture on the mountains of Israel.... I will make them lie down, says the LORD GOD. I will seek the lost, and I will bring back the strayed, and I will bind up the injured, and I will strengthen the weak. —Ezekiel 34:14-16

Readers of the New Testament, of course, will recognize these images:

> If a shepherd has a hundred sheep, and one of them has gone astray, does he not leave the ninety-nine on the mountains and go in search of the one that went astray? —Matthew 18:12

And who is this searching shepherd? "I am the good shepherd," says Jesus. "The good shepherd lays down his life for the sheep.... I am the good shepherd. I know my own and my own know me" (John 10:11-14).

All of the paintings and bulletin covers portraying Jesus as "the Good Shepherd" rework the old images that played such an important role in the life of David. David, the faithful shepherd boy and righteous shepherd king (when he was!), provides the background for understanding Jesus, who is portrayed with the same double image: the unlikely shepherd, out in the wilderness caring for "unimportant" flocks, and the glorious Shepherd King, at last establishing justice and righteousness for all the earth.

CONSIDER OTHER VOICES

East Africa

After 20-odd years of teaching psalms to seminarians, I discovered the meaning of Psalm 23 while living in East Africa in an area where it was no longer possible to rely on wealth and privilege and color. There was simply nothing in that remote village that money could buy or power coerce. My money was just dirty paper and my credit cards curious plastic artifacts. They could not save me. For food and sustenance, for care and protection, for life itself, I was completely dependent—perhaps for the first time—on God and on my African brothers and sisters, all of whom, too, were living very close to the edge of existence. I was not in control, and neither were they. I could not buy myself out. My race provided no advantage.

An awful parody of Psalm 23 sprang into my mind unbidden and found its way into my journal. It could sound arrogant, I know, but it was a confession of sin. Trust had been easy, so long as it hadn't really been necessary. But now, seeing my total dependence on something or someone other than myself, I realized how profoundly my trust had been in the wrong place—in myself and the power of my relative prosperity.

Frederick J. Gaiser

The buck's in my favor,
I shall not want.
It lets me lie down in green security;
I drink only clean waters;
it restores my soul (and my body
and my cupboard and my bank
account, and, what the heck,
I can do just about whatever
I want).
It leads me in the paths of purchasing
for my stuff's sake.
Even though I walk through the alleys
where others find death,
I fear no evil;
for my color is with me;
my wall and my locks—they
comfort me.
Wealth prepares a distance between me
and my enemies;
it anoints my mind with superiority;
my Visa runneth over.
Surely, privilege and power will follow
me all the days of my life,
and I shall dwell in the house of Dior
forever.

This, alas, had been my psalm. Not overtly, of course, and not always. But too often. Now I knew it would no longer hold. Now I knew, "The Lord is my shepherd. . . ."

BRING IT *together*

David was a shepherd boy,
He killed Golia' and shouted for joy.
Little David, play on your harp,
Hallelu, hallelu!
Little David, play on your harp, Hallelu![1]

Like our own session, the familiar black spiritual combines the two roles of David: heroic young shepherd and singer of psalms.

MEANING & RESPONSE

WHAT DOES THIS MEAN?

Psalm 28 is a prayer for help by someone who seems to be under attack, without good reason, from members of her or his own community. The psalm ends with a confession and a prayer: "The LORD is the strength of his people; he is the saving refuge of his anointed. O save your people and bless your heritage; be their shepherd, and carry them forever" (verses 8-9).

The psalm sums up many of the concerns of this session. In its confession the psalm recognizes that God's role as the "strength of his people" parallels his function as "the saving refuge of his anointed." The "anointed" one, of course, is the messianic king, the ruler on the throne of David. God exercises care for people, in part at least, through human government. Thus, in biblical perspective, the king or president or representative or school board member is called to be a faithful shepherd and servant of the people.

Finally, though, the psalm knows that the true shepherd is God. As shepherd, God carries people on his shoulder or around his neck or in his arms, just as the human shepherd cares for her sheep. This is a word of hope and comfort for us and all believers.

PLAN TO RESPOND

As we consider our response to God, the Good Shepherd, whom we meet in this session, Jesus offers his own counsel in the Gospels:

1. Follow: "I am the gate for the sheep.... The gatekeeper ... calls his own sheep by name and leads them out. When he has brought out all of his own, he goes ahead of them, and the sheep follow him because they know his voice" (John 10:7, 3-4).

2. Serve: "The good shepherd lays down his life for the sheep" (John 10:11).

3. Rejoice and tell: "Which one of you," upon finding a lost sheep, will not call together "friends and neighbors, saying to them, 'Rejoice with me, for I have found my sheep that was lost'"? (Luke 15:3-6).

Jesus calls his sheep to a life of discipleship, a life of service, and a life of joyful proclamation. This is how other people (and we ourselves) will know who and whose we are.

Think about concrete ways you act in each of these three ways. How might that work out for you in the week to come?

Continue to note the opportunities, the joys, and the frustrations of discipleship in your journal, along with other reflections on your reading and daily experience.

WORSHIP

Closing Benediction

Now may the God of peace, who brought back from the dead our Lord Jesus, the great shepherd of the sheep, by the blood of the eternal covenant, make you complete in everything good so that you may do his will, working among us that which is pleasing in his sight, through Jesus Christ, to whom be the glory forever and ever. Amen.

—Hebrews 13:20-21

1. Walter Brueggemann, *David's Truth* (Philadelphia: Fortress Press, 1985), 112.
2. "Little David, Play on Your Harp," in The Treasury of Negro Spirituals (White Plains, N.Y.: Emerson Press, 1963).

SESSION BRIDGE

LOOK BACK

- [ ] For a rich collection of text, Holy Land photographs, and art related to the life of David, look for Jerry M. Landay, *The House of David* (New York: Saturday Review Press/E. P. Dutton & Co., Inc., 1973). Text and beautiful photographs pertinent to the theme of this session can be found in Nogah Hareuveni, *Desert and Shepherd in Our Biblical Heritage* (Lod, Israel: Neot Kedumim—The Biblical Landscape Reserve in Israel, 1991).
- [ ] Continue your reading of the psalms of David. Consider using your journal to write your own psalm paraphrases. No one else need see these, of course, unless you choose, so you can be as honest in your hopes and fears, your anger and joy as are the biblical psalms themselves. If you would like to share a personal psalm or prayer with the group, opportunity will be given during the next session.

LOOK AHEAD

- [ ] Read the material in the participant book and the biblical texts (1 Kings 1 and Psalm 144) in preparation for the next session. To close out the story of David and the move to Solomon's reign, read also 1 Kings 2.
- [ ] The next session looks forward to God's fidelity to the messianic promise of 2 Samuel 7 beyond the life of David. Read some of the classic texts: Psalm 2; Isaiah 9:2-7; 11:1-9; Jeremiah 23:5-6; Micah 5:2-5a. Begin to think about how your study of David colors your reading of these promises. With this background read Matthew 21:1-16 and Acts 2:29-36.

Session SIX

the hope of PROMISE

SESSION 6

1 Kings 1:1-53;

Psalm 144:1-15

EXPERIENCES & REFLECTIONS

FOCUS David's last days as a weak old man lead us to wonder where hope finally lies in our long story. Hope emerges, however, in the God who keeps his promises, who works in every generation to establish his messianic rule. That promise comes down even to us through Jesus, the Lord's Messiah.

David Enters Jerusalem in Victory Raphael (1483–1520)

Prayer

Almighty and everlasting God, whose will it is to restore all things to your beloved Son, whom you anointed priest forever and king of all creation: Grant that all the people of the earth, now divided by the power of sin, may be united under the glorious and gentle rule of your Son, our Lord Jesus Christ, who lives and reigns with you and the Holy Spirit, one God, now and forever. Amen.[1]

NAME AND REFLECT

Who is Jesus? The New Testament uses many terms to identify him: *teacher, Son of Man, servant, rabbi, physician, beloved, Lord, friend, Son of God, king, Savior, shepherd, light, Word of God.*

When Jesus asked, "Who do people say that I am?" the disciples suggested John the Baptist, Elijah, or one of the prophets. Then Jesus heightened the issue: "But who do *you* say that I am?" And Peter answered, "You are the Messiah" (Mark 8:27-29).

The term *Messiah* (Hebrew) or *Christ* (Greek) means "the anointed one." It relates Jesus to the line of David—the anointed king whom God has promised to rule Israel. Our study of the David story helps us understand the New Testament's use of this term.

And what do *we* say? What titles or descriptions of Jesus speak most forcefully to you? How do you address Jesus in your prayers and meditation?

BRING IT *together*

After Christmas, in W. H. Auden's *For the Time Being: A Christmas Oratorio* (1944), we dismantle the tree, take down the holly and mistletoe, and get the children ready for school, all the while:

Remembering the stable where
once in our lives
Everything became a You and
nothing was an It.[2]

What does Auden mean? What is the difference between a "You" and an "It"? How does this help define God's perfect rule among us that we celebrate in Christmas and in Christ?

THE TEXT SPEAKS

START WITH THE BIBLE

The focus of this session is on 1 Kings 1 and Psalm 144. First Kings 1 cannot be read in isolation, however. It reaches back to everything in the life of David that has gone before, and it climaxes in David's death and the succession to the throne of Solomon in 1 Kings 2. Keep the earlier material in mind as you read. Go on to finish the story by reading 1 Kings 2.

EXPLORE THE TEXTS

In reading the final chapters of David's life, you may well wonder whether it was necessary for God to take such a body-strewn path on the way to establishing his messianic rule in Solomon. We probably cannot say what was "necessary" for God; we simply have the story, warts and all. With the story, we confess that God is at work through and often in spite of these historical events.

Advanced in Years

"King David was old and advanced in years." Our narrator remains brutally honest to the end. No heroic death for David. No deathbed transformations. Apparently no ability to rise above the desire for revenge. We heard the moving "last words of David" in 2 Samuel 23:1-7, but now the time of great speeches seems past. David dies as he lived: a great and powerful king, a faithful servant of Yahweh, but a deeply flawed human being, especially in affairs relating to his own family. All of the important characters meet in this final chapter, and the outcome is not pretty. Still, out of it all emerges Solomon to succeed his father on the throne. The kingdom will continue. God's promise, for one generation at least, is fulfilled.

The story of Abishag, the beautiful young woman brought after an extended search to serve as a kind of royal hot-water bottle, seems like a strange and isolated interlude. But it has greater significance: first to establish David's infirmity and the onset of a crisis of state (who will succeed the king?) and later (1 Kings 2) to heighten the tension between Solomon and Adonijah. Our narrator is nothing if not careful. Abishag comes out of nowhere, but she plays a life and death role in this story.

This brief scene itself is not without parallel. Other ancient writers speak of the attempt to transfer the warmth of a beautiful young maiden to an aging body. If this is all that is going on, Abishag is simply a nurse and a form of medicine, which is what the biblical text implies. Some writers suggest that her purpose was to restore the king's virility, to become his concubine. In either case, really, the experiment fails (1 Kings 1:4). David remains insufficiently able to exercise power, giving rise to Adonijah's grab for the throne: "I will be king" (verse 5)!

Palace Intrigue

By now, Adonijah may have been David's oldest surviving son—though we never learn the fate of his second son, Chileab (2 Samuel 3:2-5). Perhaps this, along with David's weakness, provided the motivation for Adonijah's royal coup. He quickly gains very strong support from the military and religious communities (from Joab, commander of the armies, and Abiathar, who was regularly named along with Zadok as one of the chief priests). Adonijah calls people together for an act of celebration and worship, proclaiming himself king.

The opposition is also strong, however. The other main priest, Zadok, another military leader, Benaiah, and the great prophet, Nathan, support Solomon. This nearly equal split sets the stage for civil war, especially since David seems relegated to the sidelines.

At this point, Nathan comes forward to give "advice" to Bathsheba: she should go and enlist David's support of Solomon (1 Kings 1:12). It is important to note that Nathan does not function as a prophet here. There is no indication that his "advice" is a word from God. Nathan acts as politician, a regular at court and friend of the family who is probably looking out for his own best interests. To be sure, he may well remember that God had named Solomon *Jedediah* ("beloved of the Lord," 2 Samuel 12:25), but Nathan's appeal at this dangerous moment is to *David's* oath, not to God's (1 Kings 1:13).

Bathsheba's role, too, is ambiguous. We could argue that her actions, like Nathan's, merely reflect self-interest (1 Kings 1:21). Given the willingness of members of David's family and court to kill one another, her fear is probably well taken. Still, self-interest is less than fully noble. Alternatively, we could view her as assuming the role, at last, of a more fully empowered person. She has come a long way from the young woman exploited by David when we first met her. Now she stands up for her rights and her life and those of her son. Well done!

Whatever the motives of Nathan and Bathsheba, both are, however unwittingly, making God's case—that Solomon should succeed to the throne. We can read this as another example of God's indirect hand in human affairs. The characters are allowed all of their mixed motives, but, through it all, God's will is moving its way through the story.

The characters are allowed all of their mixed motives, but, through it all, God's will is moving its way through the story.

I Have Appointed Him

The strategy of Nathan and Bathsheba works. David vows that Solomon shall succeed him as king and sends his loyal priest, Zadok, to anoint his son. We were not told whether Adonijah, as pretender to the throne, had also been anointed, though, with the priest Abiathar in his camp, that may have occurred. Now we have the explosive situation of one group shouting "Long live King Adonijah!" (verse 25) and another group shouting "Long live King Solomon!" (verse 34). The clear difference in the story (apart from the fact that Solomon has been chosen by David) is the reference to anointing, prayers, and blessings in relation to Solomon. No doubt, Adonijah's enthronement was also a religious exercise (we know, for example, that he sacrificed many animals), but the narrator does seem to attach fuller divine sanction to Solomon's ceremony.

Still, the matter is not settled. The stated authority for Solomon's rule is still only David's support (verse 35). The loose ends are real and threatening. Although Adonijah gives up his claim for the moment, his long-term plans, as we shall see, still call for his seizure of power.

Deadly Loose Ends

In stories of human pretension and palace intrigue, taking care of loose ends through violence is hardly unknown. Unhappily, our story is no exception.

Words are powerful in biblical thought.

What will become of Adonijah, Abiathar, and Joab, the three primary insurgents? At first, Adonijah seeks sanctuary at the temple (verse 51) and is granted conditional royal protection. "If wickedness is found in him," however, "he shall die" (verse 52). This is more than just a human threat. In his instructions to Solomon that begin 1 Kings 2, David reiterates the solid Deuteronomistic theology that informs the entire Old Testament: walking in God's ways and keeping his commandments brings life and blessing. But the opposite is also true: disobedience and sin result in death. In biblical theology, this is simply the way things are: obedience to God's good purposes serves life, disobedience serves death—an aspect of creation that remains true throughout the Bible and today as well.

We may be disturbed to see David, Solomon, and Benaiah serving as instruments of death for those who defied the king, but we should understand that the story involves more than merely petty and personal motives (though, alas, those are not absent). The death penalties set by the king on those guilty of treason are sentences of law, not merely personal pique.

First to fall is Adonijah, Solomon's half-brother. The basis for the death sentence is his request to marry Abishag, the beautiful young woman introduced at the beginning of our story. At one level, the request seems reasonable, even romantic. But Solomon fears more is at stake—and, indeed, royal marriages in antiquity rarely were about romance. Solomon suspects that Adonijah's grasp for Abishag, a woman associated with David, is a grasp for David's power, and therefore a new act of treason. The penalty is death. The literary connection is interesting here: Abishag appears at the beginning and end of Adonijah's insurrection. She was brought in as a source of life for David, now she becomes an occasion of death for Adonijah.

Joab must also die because of his support of Adonijah and, more obscurely, so must Shimei, because he had once cursed King David (2 Samuel 16:5-13). Words are powerful in biblical thought, and curses frequently return to plague the one who cursed.

Only when the betrayers are dead can the story end: "So the kingdom was established in the hand of Solomon" (1 Kings 2:45). This is clearly true from human perspective—Solomon is at last secure because all his opponents are gone. But there is a certain moral or theological point here, too. These deaths are the consequences of sin and serve to take away the guilt for the blood shed by the perpetrators (2 Kings 1:13). What we have here is a muddy mix of personal or political vengeance on the one hand and the assertion that the "wages of sin is death" on the other. From our later perspective, we can rightly debate the morality of vengeance and the legitimacy of capital punishment, but, no doubt, in its day, the story was wrapped up with a certain terrible tidiness.

The Lord Loved Him

The characters in our story sometimes call upon God or talk about God, but is God bound to what they say and do? Are all the terrible events in these chapters the will of God?

This narrative, along with virtually all of Scripture, makes clear that God is not responsible for disobedience and disorder. God opposes death. Even in the strong retributive theology of Deuteronomy, God's goal is certain:

> Choose life so that you and your descendants may live, loving the LORD your God, obeying him, and holding fast to him; for that means life to you and length of days, so that you may live in the land that the LORD swore to give to your ancestors, to Abraham, to Isaac, and to Jacob.
>
> —Deuteronomy 30:19b-20

So where is God in the unhappy events? The careful reader will remember that when Solomon was born, the narrator interjected an "objective" observation: "The LORD loved him" (2 Samuel 12:24). Such statements from the narrator are rare in this section of the Bible. Indeed, many commentators have noted that the genius of the David story is its honest reporting of everyday events with little theological commentary. History happens as history happens—in a kind of confusion and uncertainty that make it hard to ascribe every event to the will of God.

God is not absent though. Two texts stand out. First is the promise to David in 2 Samuel 7 that, come what may, God would establish the line of David and maintain a Davidic ruler on the throne. Second is the note that God loved Solomon. Putting these together tells us about as much as we can know about what God is doing here. Despite the human frailty of all the characters, God will remain faithful to God's promise. Despite all the terrible choices leading to Solomon's birth, God loves him. God enters human history—even a history as ambiguous and destructive as this one—in words of promise and grace.

> Say to them, As I live, says the LORD God, I have no pleasure in the death of the wicked, but that the wicked turn from their ways and live; turn back, turn back from your evil ways; for why will you die, O house of Israel?
>
> —Ezekiel 33:11

Solomon finally built the temple proposed by David.
God had established David's "house"; now Israel had a "house" for God."

Sometimes we would like to keep God out of the mix. We might want God to withdraw from stories like this one altogether. There is simply too much sin and death for God to remain on the scene. Such a desire, of course, would be self-defeating. If God stayed isolated from this messy period of history, why would God stay in ours? What would have kept him at the cross? The biblical assertion that God enters history—as it is—with grace and promise is our great hope.

The Line of David

The course of the messianic promise as it continues after the reign of Solomon is beyond the scope of this session. The recognition that the promise does continue, however, and that it culminates in Jesus of Nazareth is not. In Jesus, God enters history as surprisingly as he does in the life of David and Solomon. The trial and death of Jesus are at least as unlikely a place to find God at work as the political intrigue at David's court.

For countless generations beyond Solomon, faithful Israelites looked forward to a messianic king—a ruler who would establish God's righteousness and justice for the world. Perhaps the next child born to the royal house would be the "son given to us," the "Wonderful Counselor, Mighty God, Everlasting Father, Prince of Peace" (Isaiah 9:6). Once Jerusalem was destroyed and the monarchy broken (587 B.C.), the problem become more severe. Now what could God do?

The prophets promise new growth: "A shoot shall come out from the stump of Jesse [David's father]"—then "the wolf shall live with the lamb, the leopard shall lie down with the kid, the calf and the lion and the fatling together, and a little child shall lead them" (Isaiah 11:1-9).

Over against these expectations, the New Testament proclaims Jesus, the carpenter of Nazareth, to be God's Messiah. That was hard for people to believe. Where were the pomp and ceremony, where was the power or the transformation of the world? How could the Messiah suffer and die?

The New Testament continues to look forward to God's coming in external power, but it takes pains to assert that Jesus is the promised son of David (Matthew 1:1-17). It tells us that all the saving power and all the transforming love of God are fully present in Jesus, especially at the cross. The forgiveness of sins establishes God's kingdom in our midst. Our service of the King of kings is our service of one another and of the neighbor God gives us. The people of God join their Lord Jesus in embodying the messianic hope for the world.

And Now What Are Human Beings?

With Psalm 144, we come full circle back to the question of Psalm 8: "What are human beings that you regard them, or mortals that

"A shoot shall come from the root of Jesse" (Isaiah 11:1).

you think of them?" (verse 3). The answer is different now. Psalm 8 seemed young and idealistic, celebrating the creative possibilities of human beings who were "little less than the angels." But time has passed. David's idealistic youth have given way to the sins of his mid-life crisis and his failures in familial and state affairs. It is hard to be so optimistic. What are human beings? "They are like a breath," says Psalm 144, "their days are like a passing shadow" (verse 4).

> Life's but a walking shadow,
>   a poor player
> That struts and frets his hour
>   upon the stage
> And then is heard no more; it is a tale
> Told by an idiot, full of sound and fury,
> Signifying nothing.[3]
>
> —William Shakespeare

It is hard to count on human achievement now. Without God, hope will be hard to come by.

Happy Are the People Whose God Is the Lord

Still, Psalm 144 does not give up—not on hope, not on happiness, not on human beings, not on God. "Happy are the people whose God is the LORD" (verse 15). With God, renewal is possible. The future can look bright again.

The psalmist prays for God to come and restore the people. And when that happens? We will sing again (verse 9). We will live in prosperity (verses 12-14). We will be happy (verse 15).

Notice the move in the psalm from the first verse to the last. In verse 1, the psalmist blesses the Lord. In verse 15, the Lord blesses people. This is not some calculated deal: Let's see, if I say nice things about God he will be nice to me. It is a true and living relationship in which my happiness comes from blessing God and God's happiness comes in blessing us.

Despite human failure, the psalm does not give up on humans: May our sons and daughters be strong. May our barns be filled. May our cities be safe (verses 12-14). Life prospers as humans work under the blessing of God, with trust in God. The Bible does not guarantee worldly success for believers, but it does promise meaningful and hopeful life for those who know God.

In Christ, God's blessings are strikingly new. God "gives victory to kings" and "rescues his servant David," sings the psalm (verse 10). In the New Testament, we know that Jesus is the servant king rescued by God on Easter morning. That new life becomes a gift to all of us, defeating sin, death, and the devil once and for all. Now, in a whole new way, "happy are the people whose God is the Lord."

CONSIDER OTHER VOICES

American writer Stephen Vincent Benét wrote a cynical poem entitled "King David" in 1923. Whether clear to the author of not, beneath Benét's dim view of David lies a theological perspective close to that of the biblical story itself, where God works through a very messy period of history to establish the line of David. Here are some of Benét's lines:

> David sang to his hook-nosed harp:
>
> "The Lord God is a jealous God!
> His violent vengeance is swift and
>   sharp!
> And the Lord is King above all gods!
>
> "Blest be the Lord, through years
>   untold,
> The Lord Who blessed me a
>   thousand fold!
>
> "Cattle and concubines, corn and hives
> Enough to last me a dozen lives
>
> . . . .
>
> "I wax in His peace like a pious gourd,
> The Lord God is a pleasant God,
> Break mine enemy's jaw, O Lord!
> For the Lord is King above all gods!"

Following a lengthy (and rather vicious) account of the incident with Bathsheba and Uriah and the death of the child, Benét has David return to Bathsheba, now his wife:

"The justice of God is honey and balm.
I will soothe her heart with a little
psalm."
He went to her chamber, no longer
sad,
Walking as light as a shepherd lad.
He found her weeping, her garments
rent,
Trodden like straw by God's
punishment.
He solaced her out of his great content.

. . . .

Nine months later she bore him a son.
(The Lord God is a mighty God!)
The name of that child was
SOLOMON.
He was God's tough staff till his days
were run!
(And the Lord is King above all gods!)[4]

How shall we understand Benét's refrain that the Lord is "a mighty God" and "King above all gods," even though he seems to allow David to get away with murder? Is the poem agnostic, talking of God but really thinking God had nothing to do with these events? Is the author merely cynical, ascribing "greatness" to a God who seems more like a monster? Or can we hear the Bible's own theological undercurrent, affirming God's action in and through historical events, even though neither God nor the biblical narrator approved of many of the events themselves?

BRING IT *together*

When John heard in prison what the Messiah was doing, he sent word by his disciples and said to him, "Are you the one who is to come, or are we to wait for another?" Jesus answered them, "Go and tell John what you hear and see: the blind receive their sight, the lame walk, the lepers are cleansed, the deaf hear, the dead are raised, and the poor have good news brought to them. And blessed is anyone who takes no offense at me."

—Matthew 11:2-6

How do we know that Jesus is the promised Messiah? John the Baptist asked the same question. Jesus' response has a double meaning. On the one hand, it points to the healing and new life that mark the kingdom of God. On the other hand, it recalls specific Old Testament promises that are now being fulfilled. Jesus is the fulfillment of the promise. Jesus is the source of healing and life. This is the Messiah.

MEANING & RESPONSE

WHAT DOES THIS MEAN?

How shall we know what God is doing in the world? The story of David and the story of Jesus remind us that the answer is not easy. God works in strange ways, participating in events of human history that sometimes seem unredeemable. What is the key to finding God's work and God's will?

According to Martin Luther, the answer comes in trusting God's Word of law and promise. Seeking the God hidden in history and creation apart from God's revealed Word is fruitless and dangerous.

> What He [the hidden God] is, what He does, and what His will is does not concern me. But this does concern me, that I know what He has commanded, what He has promised, and what He has threatened. When you reflect on these things carefully, you find God, yes, He Himself takes you on His lap. If you fall out of it, that is, if you presume to know anything beyond what has been revealed in the Word, you plunge into the depths of hell.[5]

As we look at our world and into ourselves, trying to learn what God is doing, we cannot avoid the awful questions of "why" and "how long" and "where" and "when." These were the questions of the lament psalms and continue to be our questions as well. We can certainly ask them of this strange and wonderful story of David.

Luther reminds us to avoid trying to find the answers on our own. We are in over our heads and the quest may well damage our spiritual health. Health comes from hearing and trusting God's word. From the David story, that would include the word of command, calling David and Solomon and us to obedience that we and others might live full and abundant lives, and the word of promise, establishing justice and righteousness in God's messianic kingdom—amid all the terrors and ambiguities of human history.

PLAN TO RESPOND

God's anointing of David and Solomon as kings of Israel led eventually to the anointing of Jesus as the messianic king of all creation. We, too, have been anointed in our baptism and set free to do God's work in the world.

Our anointing to the service of God is plain, for example, in the Lutheran rite of Holy Baptism. As the baptized person is anointed with oil, the minister says:

> ___Name___, child of God, you have been sealed by the Holy Spirit and marked with the cross of Christ forever.

Then a lighted candle is given to the baptized, and a representative of the congregation says:

> Let your light so shine before others that they may see your good works and glorify your Father in heaven.[6]

Just before the anointing in the Roman Catholic celebration of Baptism and Confirmation for adults, the celebrant says:

> My dear friends, let us pray to God our Father, that he will pour out the Holy Spirit on these newly baptized to strengthen them with his gifts and anoint them to be more like Christ, the Son of God.[7]

In what ways can we open ourselves more fully to let our "light shine before others"? How will we become "more like Christ"? Talk about this with your group, seeking concrete ways to respond in your own families, congregations, and community.

WORSHIP

As a star, God's holy Word
Leads us to our King and Lord;
Brightly from its sacred pages
Shall this light throughout the ages
Shine upon our path of life,
Shine upon our path of life.

—Nikolai Grundtvig, 1783–1872

---

1. "Prayer of the Day for Christ the King," *Lutheran Book of Worship* (Minneapolis: Augsburg, 1978), 30.
2. "For the Time Being" in the *Collected Works of W. H. Auden* (New York: Random House, 1945), 466.
3. MacBeth in *The Complete Works of William Shakespeare* (Garden City: Doubleday, 1936), 1053.
4. "King David" in *Selected Works of Stephen Vincent Benét: Volume One, Poetry* (New York: Farrar and Rinehart, 1942).
5. *Luther's Works*, vol. 3, *Lectures on Genesis Chapters 15-20* (St. Louis: Concordia, 1961), 139.
6. Holy Baptism Rubrics 14-16, *Lutheran Book of Worship* (Minneapolis: Augsburg, 1978), 124.
7. *Rite of Christian Initiation of Adults* (Collegeville: The Order of St. Benedict, Inc., 1988), 146.

Bridge

SESSION BRIDGE

LOOK BACK

- ☐ Continue or complete your reading of the psalms of David. One way the psalms have been read by believers and historians is in connection with particular events in David's life. Think about this in your own reading of the psalms—not just to establish their place in "objective" history but as a way to apply them to similar situations in your own life. As the "son of David," the psalms also become the prayers of Jesus. As you read the psalms, think of them as Jesus' prayers. You can get help in this from Dietrich Bonhoeffer, *Psalms: The Prayer Book of the Bible* (Minneapolis: Augsburg, 1970).
- ☐ As another way to review the life of David, look for the recent Broadway musical, *King David,* by Alan Menken and Tim Rice (a Disney production).
- ☐ If you have kept a journal during this study, reread what you have written. It is often surprising how we can be fed by our own words—which is one reason to consider continuing or beginning the journaling process. Some people like to "journal" on a computer, precisely because it allows them to search more easily for ideas they vaguely remember recording but not quite recalling where or when.

LOOK AHEAD

- ☐ Will another Inspire course follow this one? If so, ask your leader about enrolling and getting the books to prepare for Session 1 in that course. Or what other opportunities for Bible study are available in your congregation? Perhaps you would like to expand your knowledge by becoming involved in one of them.
- ☐ Is it time for you to become a local Bible study leader? Think about this as a way to extend your own learning and to be of service to others. Ask about what training and preparation are available for leaders of Inspire or other Bible studies.
- ☐ Christians are nourished by regular study of the Bible. Even if you are not quickly moving to another formal study, try to find a disciplined way to read and study on your own. Ask your leader or pastor for programs that are designed for this. You can always plan to work through a particular book of the Bible, using the helps provided in a study Bible. Bible dictionaries, commentaries, and concordances will be available in your congregational or community library.